A LITTLE BIT OF

LUCID
DREAMING

A LITTLE BIT OF

LUCID DREAMING

AN INTRODUCTION TO DREAM MANIPULATION

CYRENA LEE

STERLING ETHOS
New York

STERLING ETHOS
New York

An Imprint of Sterling Publishing Co., Inc.
122 Fifth Avenue
New York, NY 10011

Text © 2020 Cyrena Lee
Cover © 2020 Sterling Publishing Co., Inc.

ISBN 978-1-4549-4284-9

Distributed in Canada by Sterling Publishing Co., Inc.
c/o Canadian Manda Group, 664 Annette Street
Toronto, Ontario M6S 2C8, Canada
Distributed in the United Kingdom by GMC Distribution Services
Castle Place, 166 High Street, Lewes, East Sussex BN7 1XU, England
Distributed in Australia by NewSouth Books
University of New South Wales, Sydney, NSW 2052, Australia

For information about custom editions, special sales, and premium and corporate purchases,
please contact Sterling Special Sales at 800-805-5489 or specialsales@sterlingpublishing.com.

Manufactured in the United States of America

2 4 6 8 10 9 7 5 3

sterlingpublishing.com

Interior design by Shannon Nicole Plunkett
Cover design by Elizabeth Mihaltse Lindy

Image Credits
Shutterstock (cover, throughout): Peratek (hands); satit_srihin (border)

CONTENTS

INTRODUCTION:
LUCID DREAMING

Lucid dreaming, simply put, is the realization that you are dreaming. To lucid dream is to wake up *inside* a dream. To be lucid is to be aware and to know that everything you see before you is a product of your own imagination and consciousness. To be lucid is to marvel at the world before your eyes, and to delight in the freedom of your actions. And being lucid in a dream is just the beginning—from there, you can really take control of your dream.

I can't remember where I first heard of the concept of "lucid dreaming"; perhaps I stumbled upon it somewhere on the internet. But I was intrigued by the possibility that we could control an entire world while sleeping: we could bend and defy the laws of physics and gravity; manifest any animal or the sun in a blazing purple sky instead of a blue one; face our monsters, knowing that they were only reflections of our fears, and thus powerless. The only limit in the dream world is our own imagination. Anything we can think of is possible.

Lucid dreaming can be therapeutic. It can rewrite the script of past traumas. It can stimulate creativity for artists and even help athletes with their physical pursuits. It can deepen self-understanding. But the single most important life lesson I've learned has been from my adventures into lucid dreaming: To the mind, there is little difference between the dream world and the real world. To take control of your waking life, and to live a life you've always wanted, you just have to learn how to dream it.

As a young child, I'd always dreamt of being a writer. For the past twenty years or so, I have obsessively kept daily journals and dream journals. And for the past five years, I've intensely researched and read all about lucid dreaming and how to do it, and have talked at length with friends, family, and strangers about their dreams. Learning how to lucid dream has changed my life drastically, because it helped me learn how to change my life. In the past few years, thanks to lucid dreaming, I've managed to walk away from a soul-draining career at a slew of start-ups. I've learned to overcome limitations to pursue my longtime dream of writing books and novels that help me connect with others, and help them realize the power of their own imaginations. It's led me to this very moment in writing these words, and to this very moment of you reading these words. The best thing about lucid dreaming is that anyone can learn how to do it, no matter who they are and what their circumstances. At the same time, anyone can learn how to live lucidly.

You don't need to buy that ability or possess anything but the will to hold a belief in order to lucid dream. The goal of this book is to get you not only lucid dreaming, but to also live your life lucidly. Let's begin.

❖ 1 ❖

WHAT IS A LUCID DREAM?

"What is a television apparatus to man, who has only to shut his eyes to see the most inaccessible regions of the seen and the never seen, who has only to imagine in order to pierce through walls and cause all the planetary Baghdads of his dreams to rise from the dust."

—SALVADOR DALÍ

WHAT HAPPENS WHEN WE FALL ASLEEP? With our jam-packed schedules, how often do we think about our dreams? What hope can we have to change our future for the better if we don't remember our dreams? How much time have we spent thinking about television shows or the lives of celebrities instead of probing our own imaginations?

In a society that values constant productivity and connectivity, sleep is often given short shrift. Of course, trendy wellness businesses try to capitalize on consumer insecurities to "optimize" sleep, by encouraging us to buy the perfect mattress or silk pajama set. You may have even seen a travel advertisement for a weekend away to "disconnect"—but few of us think about what actually happens when we disconnect and sleep. Very little attention is paid to the fact that we all dream, and that lucid dreams exist.

All of us, more or less, exist in this fever dream of consumerism, where we are forced to work to make money. And, with our money, we buy things that are marketed to us, to try to fill our needs. Sadly, most of the products that are peddled to us either make us sick (junk food, bad television), make the environment sick (plastics and other unnecessary objects that pollute the planet), or make us pay to be healthy (vitamins and juice cleanses). But dreams are free, even if they are often scoffed at, and every person who sleeps also dreams. We are all awake every day, and are highly conscious of our own ideas. We know our limitations, what we can and cannot do, what is and is not possible, who we are and who we are not.

But in the dream world we can break free of these limitations. Children are often adept at lucid dreaming, likely because they don't yet have any preconceptions about what is and is not possible. In dreams, anything is possible. In the dream world, we can fly with no regard to gravity, we can teleport ourselves from one place to the next, levitate objects, invent new colors, and even embody animals or other people. Sometimes our dreams are less pleasant. Perhaps you find yourself with recurring anxiety-inducing dreams that make you feel helpless, like the horror of your teeth crumbling in your mouth, or the desperation of being unable to outrun a monster, or the futility and terror of steering an out-of-control car. Or perhaps you don't remember your dreams at all, or think that you don't dream. But one scientific study conducted in 2015 by French scientists affirms that "dreaming production is universal," as is the ability to lucid dream. A German study from 2011 even found that more than half of the population already had experienced a lucid dream at least once!

So what, exactly, is a lucid dream? A lucid dream simply refers to a dream in which you are aware that you are dreaming. *Lucidity* can be defined as the practice of clearly grasping your thoughts and making them easily understood, or the practice of thinking and speaking clearly. Thus, to have a lucid dream is to clearly understand the situation at hand: to recognize a dream for what it is, and the fact that you are in it.

When we go to sleep, we cycle through four different stages. The first three are classified as NREM (non–rapid eye movement) sleep, and the fourth is called the REM (rapid eye movement) cycle; this is where dreaming occurs. Our eyeballs are actually moving during the REM stage of sleep because we are looking around in our dream environment. During the first stage, the body is just drifting off to sleep and can be awakened by loud noises or other disruptions, while brain waves slow down. In the second stage of sleep, the body temperature starts to drop while the heart rate begins to slow. The third stage of NREM sleep is the deepest and most restorative, while the brain produces delta waves (or slow waves). This is followed by the fourth stage of sleep, known as REM sleep, in which the eyes rapidly move back and forth and brain-wave activity jumps up again.

During this sleep cycle, most of the body becomes paralyzed, except the eyelids and the lungs (for obvious reasons). A person can have anywhere from four to six dreams a night during this stage.

One researcher at the Federal University of Rio Grande do Norte in Brazil observed increased alpha brain waves—the waves usually associated with being awake but with closed eyes—during lucid REM sleep. Therefore, the lucid dream state is one in which the dreamer is, in a sense, awake. Another study, conducted in 2009 at Frankfurt University in Germany, observed that there was an increase in gamma waves and coherence during lucid dreams. Gamma waves, the rarest type of brain waves, are also produced during meditation. With gamma waves, information is passed rapidly and quietly, and these brain waves are also highly active during states of universal love and a oneness with nature. Exactly how gamma waves are generated is a mystery—much like the origins of dreams.

Some people mistakenly believe that lucid dreaming implies full dream control; in actuality, there are various levels of lucidity. Generally speaking, we can group lucidity into five different levels of intensity.

LEVEL ONE-In the first level of lucidity, you have a basic awareness that you are dreaming. In this level, you may wake up in a dream and realize that you are asleep, but you simply observe and go along with what is happening in the dream.

LEVEL TWO-The second level of lucidity involves having a conscious, but perhaps shaky, hold on dream manipulation and action; for example, jumping up to fly, walking through walls, or trying to talk to your dream characters. These actions may prove difficult, and you may lose control easily and revert back to the first level.

LEVEL THREE-In the third level of lucidity, you consciously manipulate your dream on a large scale by changing the scenery, altering the script, or materializing people or objects in front of you.

LEVEL FOUR-At the fourth level of lucidity, you exert full dream control. Here, you are able to incubate dreams with intention before going to sleep. This means you can guide and even program the content of your dream before you even fall asleep. Once you're in the dream, you can then comfortably control the events as they proceed.

LEVEL FIVE-The fifth level of lucid dreaming refers to going beyond the dream world by meditating inside your dream and experiencing a sacred connectedness.

❀ ❀ ❀

The funny thing about dreaming is that when you're in a dream, it feels just as real as everyday waking life. But when you become lucid and recognize that you have the freedom to do whatever you wish in this dream—with no restrictions, judgments, or ramifications—it is thrilling. To realize that you are in complete control—that you have the freedom to go anywhere in your dreamscape or even change the scenes before you at will—is to recognize that you are in full control of your dream destiny. But, for me, the real magic of lucid dreaming occurs when this beautiful awareness of how your mental state reflects and changes a dream crosses over to your waking life: With lucid dreaming, you'll be able to begin lucid living.

A BRIEF HISTORY OF LUCID DREAMING

*"How much the imagination creates wonderful spectacles
when it rules in absolute sovereignty, freed from what life
demands of progress and barriers, without any reserve
left to all the delights of the ideal!"*

—MARQUIS D'HERVEY DE SAINT-DENYS

E VER SINCE THE TIMES OF ANCIENT CIVILIZA-
tions, such as those thriving in Mesopotamia, Egypt,
Greece, and Rome, people have been interested in dreams
and in interpreting their meanings. Over two thousand years ago,
in his work *On Dreams*, the Greek philosopher Aristotle hinted at
the possibility of being aware that one is in a sleeping state. The
first written record of the concept of lucid dreaming appeared in
1867, in a book on dreaming written by Marquis d'Hervey de Saint-
Denys—*Les rêves et les moyens de les diriger; observations pratiques
(Dreams and the Ways to Direct Them: Practical Observations)*. But

it wasn't until 1975 that lucid dreaming was proved to be true in a pioneering experiment conducted by British psychologist Dr. Keith Hearne. The subject of the experiment, Alan Worsley, was asleep in a chair and sent deliberate signals that were recorded on a polygraph machine while he was in his dream state. It was a landmark experiment that was later famously repeated by American psychophysiologist and lucid dream researcher Stephen LaBerge in 1980. However, the news of such an incredible discovery—receiving a message from a person in a completely different world, the "dream world"—traveled slowly in the pre-internet days. But before we dive into the recent history of lucid dreaming, let us look at the foundation of dreams and what they've symbolized throughout history.

LUCID DREAMING IN ANTIQUITY

Egyptians considered dreams to be of divine origin, and messages decoded from dreams influenced important political decisions and helped to cure illnesses. There were even specially educated temple priests, called Masters of the Secret Things, to help interpret dreams. Lasting proof is found in the artifact *The Egyptian Dream Book*, which dates back to around 1279–1213 BCE. Housed at the British Museum, the book is made out of papyrus and lists a number of dreams and their interpretations. So powerful was the potential of dreams for the Egyptians that they even enacted rituals to "incubate" their dreams—an early form of dream control. The ancient burial ground of Saqqara was an important healing center in the late third century BCE, where individuals would participate in rituals to initiate a dream in which cures would be revealed.

In the second century CE, professional diviner Artemidorus wrote *Oneirocritica (The Interpretation of Dreams)*, an ancient Greek treatise on dream interpretation. This is where the term oneironaut comes from, meaning "one who has the ability to travel within a dream consciously." Two centuries later, lucid dreaming was first mentioned in writing in 415 CE, by Saint Augustine, in a letter he penned to Saint Evodius in 415 CE. In it, he describes the intriguing lucid dream of a Roman physician named Gennadius. In Gennadius's dream, he is visited by a young man who brings him to a city where a wonderful melody fills the streets. In a subsequent dream, the young man asks Gennadius to recount to him where they had met before and even prompted him to realize that he was now "seeing in sleep."

In the Eastern world, Tibetan Buddhists have been engaging in lucid dream practices since at least the eighth century. Eminent Tibetan lama Tenzin Wangyal Rinpoche describes *dream yoga*—also known as milam—as potential for a spiritual journey, and says that, "Normally, the dream is thought to be 'unreal,' as opposed to 'real' waking life. But there is nothing more real than a dream. This statement only makes sense once it is understood that normal waking life is as unreal as a dream, and in exactly the same way." For the Tibetan Buddhists, the pursuit of understanding the dream world and the ultimate goal of dream yoga is complete awakening, known as enlightenment. Enlightenment allows practitioners to awaken from samsara—the interminable cycle of life, matter, and existence. The 2012 documentary of the same name, *Samsara*, captures this concept with incredibly powerful images of the modern world, filmed in over twenty-five countries. Arresting images of factory hands, of chickens and pigs being processed, of breathtaking nature scenes, and of developing-country slums blaze across the screen. For many of us, life can seem like a never-ending scroll of images and scenes that happen to us. Lucid dreaming is a practice that helps us take control.

LUCID DREAMING IN MODERNITY

Samsara can also be used to describe the daily repetition of mundane tasks that occupy most of our lives: waking up, checking our social media and email, brushing our teeth, eating our breakfast, taking public transportation, going to work, eating the same lunch at the same time each day, taking a coffee break, fighting boredom in meetings, going back home, eating dinner, feeling exhausted and disappointed that we didn't have enough time to do what we really wanted, watching TV or surfing the internet—before falling back to sleep, only to wake up and do the same thing all over again. Sometimes, life can feel like a boring dream, or even a nightmare that is an endless cycle of these repetitive and mundane tasks.

What lucid dreaming offers is an escape from this cycle, and modern dream explorers of the last century and a half have broken a lot of ground for the lucid dreamers of tomorrow.

Here's a brief outline of some of the most important developments in and work done on dreams and lucid dreaming since the late nineteenth century. (All of the selected works are highly recommended for further reading.)

1867—Marquis d'Hervey de Saint-Denys publishes *Les rêves et les moyens de les diriger; observations pratiques (Dreams and the Ways to Direct Them: Practical Observations)*, and coins the term lucid dreaming.

1900—Sigmund Freud publishes the highly influential book *The Interpretation of Dreams*, which significantly impacts dream theory by stating that all dreams are caused by our desires for "wish fulfillment," or the desire to destroy the wish.

1913—Dutch psychiatrist Frederik Willem van Eeden presents a paper, called "A Study of Dreams," to a meeting of the Society for Psychical Research. He reports 352 of his own lucid dreams and the experiments he has done while lucid.

1921—Englishwoman Mary Arnold-Forster publishes *Studies in Dreams* at the age of sixty, and brazenly disagrees with the popular Freudian theory that dreams are symbolic. Her book focuses on dream control, voluntary dreaming, the "super-dream" (her name for lucid dreaming), dream characters, and more.

1936—Alward Embury Brown publishes a paper called "Dreams in Which the Dreamer Knows He Is Asleep" in the *Journal of Abnormal Psychology*. He describes his own lucid dreams to demonstrate that lucid dreaming is a different state from regular dreaming.

1939—Englishman Hugh Callaway, a proficient lucid dreamer, publishes a book called *Astral Projection* under the pen name of Oliver Fox. Other than astral projection, the other pathway to an out-of-body experience is described as "dream awakening."

1952—Rapid eye movement, or the REM cycle, is discovered at the University of Chicago by Eugene Aserinsky and Nathaniel Kleitman. This breakthrough discovery paves the way for more research because the sleep state was previously considered a passive state.

1968—Celia Green publishes *Lucid Dreams*, in which she predicts that lucid dreams would be found to correlate with rapid eye movement sleep (later confirmed by British psychologist Dr. Keith Hearne).

1975—A landmark experiment conducted by British psychologist Dr. Keith Hearne proves the existence of lucid dreaming to be true, using his ocular-signaling technique with subject Alan Worsley.

1976—Scott Sparrow publishes *Lucid Dreaming: Dawning of the Clear Light*. This is the first major book on the subject published in North America, and it was so popular the publishers asked him to update it in 2014.

1981—Stephen LaBerge successfully replicates Dr. Hearne's experiment in his own study, "Lucid Dream Verified by Volitional Communication during REM Sleep," which has sleepers signal pre-agreed-upon eye movements from a dream state.

1983—The International Association for the Study of Dreams (IASD) is founded and hosts its first annual conference. The nonprofit and international organization is dedicated to the "pure and applied investigation of dreams and dreaming."

1993—Anthropologist Carlos Castaneda publishes *The Art of Dreaming*, which details his apprenticeship with a Mexican Yaqui Indian sorcerer, Don Juan Matus. He calls dreaming the "gateway to infinity."

2009—A study conducted by the Sleep Laboratory of the Neurological Clinic in Frankfurt discovers a significant increase in brain activity during lucid dreams, distinguishing them from regular dreaming. Brain-wave frequencies during lucid dreams were recorded in the gamma range, which are far higher than the normal dream state, composed of theta waves.

2017—MIT launches the Dream Lab, where a team of researchers study sleep states and how to develop technologies to "access the unique, imaginative, elastic cognition ongoing during dreams and semi-lucid states."

❧ ❧ ❧

With the advent of easily accessible pop culture and the internet, lucid dreaming has made its way from obscure and ancient texts, niche research fields, and New Age spiritual books to the mainstream, thanks to movies like *Paprika* (2006) and *Inception* (2010). *Paprika* is a

Japanese science-fiction, psychological thriller that takes place across dreams that eventually merge into reality. It inspired the popular American film *Inception*, which features incredible scenes of dreams being constructed and then falling apart. As of now, there are around 23 million results in Google for the term *lucid dream*. If you want to learn more about lucid dreaming, there are countless TED talks on lucid dreaming, YouTube how-to videos, and hundreds of books and blogs about dreaming yourself awake. Another fine example of a once–somewhat esoteric concept that's now everywhere is the sleeper hit "Lucid Dreams" by the late artist Juice WRLD. In the song, he raps about having lucid dreams, but how he is unable to move any-thing in them, which is a poetic description of being aware of a situ-ation, and yet being unable to master it. This lyric is also reflective of the lucid dream concept in society: Many of us know what it is, but do we really know how to move and control our dreams?

While many philosophers have agonized over the meaning and function of dreams, and scientists have tried to find the exact source and practical mechanism behind dreams (scientists have yet to dis-cover where dreams come from), many artists, athletes, and thera-pists have used dreams and lucidity within the dream state to great benefit: to tackle nightmares, for self-discovery, to improve athletic skill, to unblock artistic creativity, and more. But most people ignore their dreams, rather than exploring the possibility of directing them.

I've always found it rather sad that society, and especially parents, often dismiss the fanciful tales or nightmares children recount over breakfast as "mere dreams." Why is it that we consider television, online news sites, and social media feeds more reliable and important sources of "reality" than what we would see if we looked inward, toward the incredible projections of our own consciousness, which we each experience every night? Fortunately, it is never too late to pay attention to our dreams, nor is it ever too late to begin to lucid dream.

The Future of Lucid Dreaming

The one upside of living in the digital age is that now, more than ever, people have greater access to materials and resources and the opportunity to exchange ideas. While the 24/7 news cycle and the pressure to live in an ever-connected, always-on world are sources of stress in contemporary life, we are also living at a time when we can access any information we want, so we can live any kind of life that we wish. Technology has also brought us devices to help facilitate lucid dreaming or, depending on how you look at it, devices to sell our dreams back to us. On Kickstarter alone, there have been at least four high-tech lucid dreaming accessories that launched in the last decade, such as the LucidCatcher wristband, the Aurora Dreamband, the Neuroon mask, and the iBand EEG headband. These expensive gadgets all claim to help induce lucid dreaming and to track brain waves during sleep. Whether or not these accessories work is yet to be proved, but one 2014 study gives hope to technology-induced lucid dreaming. Dream researcher Ursula Voss and her team discovered that a 40-hertz electrical stimulation of the scalp during REM sleep "triggered lucidity in 77 percent of the time." What is even more surprising about this study is that none of these subjects had previously experienced a lucid dream before, demonstrating the true potential for advanced technology to bring lucid dreaming to the masses.

Inception does not seem too far-fetched, either. As of this writing, in 2020, the team of researchers at MIT's Dream Lab announced the development of an "open source wearable device that can track and interact with dreams in a number of ways." Their glovelike device, the Dormio, senses which state the sleeper is in and then plays an audio clip during the hypnogogic state. Depending on the audio cue, the sleeper can hypothetically insert different dream topics into the actual dream.

Meanwhile, researchers in Japan are working on visualizing dreams through technology. In 2013, neuroscientist Yukiyasu Kamitani recorded brain waves of hundreds of nappers, and had a computer program turn the basic contents of their dreams into short videos. Astonishingly, the study "found these were 70 percent accurate compared with what subjects remembered of their real dreams." Other new technologies will potentially be able to record body movements during dreams and perhaps even speech during dreams. Some lucid dreamers may become movie directors in the future.

❄ ❄ ❄

All these advances in dream technology have one goal in common: to help people control and direct their dreams. However, I firmly believe that anyone can lucid dream without spending a lot of money on expensive technology. All of us can learn to lucid dream on our own, and many lucid dreamers find that dream control ends up being a tool that is helpful for almost every aspect in life. In short, learning to control your dreams can help you gain control over your own waking life. While dreams, as a mystic realm, have been a subject of human interest for thousands and thousands of years, only recently has lucid dreaming become scientifically proven and central to the public consciousness. The possibilities of lucid dreaming are limitless, and even if the history of lucid dreaming is relatively recent—it is an exciting time, because it's just begun.

❖ 3 ❖

WHY LUCID DREAM?

"*Basically, at the very bottom of life, which seduces us all,
there is only absurdity, and more absurdity. And maybe that's
what gives us our joy for living, because the only thing
that can defeat absurdity is lucidity.*"

—ALBERT CAMUS

PERHAPS YOU'RE A REALIST AND THINK THAT THE world of "reality" is far more important than the dream world. Perhaps you scoff at people who believe in "woo-woo" things like spirits, ghosts, astro-travel, or dream worlds. But to quote Yuval Noah Harari, author of *Sapiens: A Brief History of Humankind*, "People easily understand that 'primitives' cement their social order by believing in ghosts and spirits, and gathering each full moon to dance together around the campfire. What we fail to appreciate is that our modern institutions function on exactly the same basis. Take for example the world of business corporations.

Modern business-people and lawyers are, in fact, powerful sorcerers. The principal difference between them and tribal shamans is that modern lawyers tell far stranger tales." Since most of the structures of the "real" world began as a mere dream or idea in somebody's head, there's a strong argument in favor of paying attention to the possibility of your own dream world. Or say you're more of a glass-half-empty type of person, who likes to point out the negative aspects or downside of everything—perhaps you worry that if you venture into the lucid dreaming realm, the quality of your sleep will deteriorate. Since lucid dreaming occurs during the REM cycle of sleep (REM meaning "rapid eye movement," which happens to be the only part of the body, except the lungs, not paralyzed by the dream state), your brain is registering the same level of activity, whether you're aware of being in the dream state or not. So whether or not you are conscious that you are dreaming does not leave you more tired in the morning.

Others have worried that if lucid dreaming is such a thrilling experience, some may sink into the dream world, only never to return to "reality." As a lucid dreamer myself, I can only say that the more one ventures into the dream world and dream consciousness, the more one realizes that there is actually very little difference between the dream world and the real world. Each one is a reflection of the other. The real world can be just as surprising, unpredictable, absurd, and magical as the dream world. Strange coincidences and wild synchronicities occur all the time in both worlds. We can experience lucid living just as we experience lucid dreaming, but because the dream world is not circumscribed by the limits of gravity or the perception of time, it is far easier to begin there to remove our own limitations and experience absolute freedom and creativity. Anyone can benefit from lucid dreaming, from people who simply want to get to know themselves a bit better or to stop a recurring nightmare, to athletes who wish to improve their skills on the playing field, people who are sick and are looking for complementary and holistic ways of healing, and artists of all kinds who wish to unlock their creativity.

SELF-DISCOVERY

Sometimes when people talk about their dreams, they may use the term *dream* in a more literal sense: They dream of one day becoming a famous football player or a highly respected doctor, or of creating a music festival, or of helping others. You can tell a lot about people from their dreams. But where exactly do these dreams—these ideas of what we want to do with our life—come from? Sometimes we may be born into certain lives or paths, with a lot of pressure to act a certain way, to take on the family business, to carry on traditions, or to conform to societal expectations of what we should do in life. We are primed to live within the strictures of the outer world and what people expect of us, and we look to what has already been done in the waking world to see what is possible. But by paying attention to our dreams at night, we can learn a lot about ourselves and what we truly desire—not what society or others tell us to want. Dreams can carry important messages when we're off track, if we are not living in sync with our desires. If we are acting in a self-sabotaging way, or if we have never gotten over some past trauma, focusing on our dreams can help us heal and course-correct.

SEXUAL LIBERATION AND HEALING

Perhaps you're in a bit of a sexual rut, or are too afraid to experiment with your sexuality for fear of others' judgment. In the dream world, you have the absolute freedom to do whatever with whomever you want, with no repercussions or risks of real-world ramifications, like sexually transmitted diseases or pregnancy. Most beginner lucid dreamers engage in lucid dreaming sex because it can be outrageously gratifying—imagine having any partner you wish, fictional or real, and deriving real pleasure from it; that is, real pleasure that carries over to your waking body. In 1983, at the Stanford Sleep Lab, Beverly D'Urso proved the possibility of lucid dream–induced orgasm during an experiment conducted by Stephen LaBerge. Beverly was hooked up to electrodes and vaginal probes, and dreamt about flying over the Stanford campus, where a group of tourists was walking below. After she chose a man in a blue suit as her partner, she signaled to the real world at the beginning of the act and once again before orgasming. This first recorded female orgasm achieved in a dream state was chronicled in the *Journal of Psychophysiology*. In addition to sexual liberation, lucid dreaming has proven therapeutic for those who may have experienced sexual trauma or developed sexual blockages.

STOPPING NIGHTMARES

For those with recurring nightmares or anxiety dreams, becoming lucid is a direct way to deal with the issue underlying those nightmares. Most people who have the same distressing dream night after night are usually ignoring a huge issue in their life. Becoming lucid not only forces you to pay attention to what is actually happening in your life, it also prompts you to change the outcome so that you can resolve a persistent problem. With a lucid mind, you can approach your threatening dream figure and confront it, perhaps even ask it what it wants from you. People who face their fears in dreams may find that the figure they had imagined to be so threatening and terrifying will often shrink and lose its power, or give a reason for why it is there, and thus offer insight into your problem. Other times, by confronting the fears in your dream, you can tell yourself, when you're lucid, that it is just a dream—that you really haven't lost your teeth, that you aren't naked in front of a bunch of people. This realization can help ease your anxiety.

SLEEP PARALYSIS

If you've already lived through an episode of sleep paralysis, then you know the universal feeling of terror associated with it all too well. If you aren't familiar with it, sleep paralysis occurs between the phases of being awake and asleep. If you are experiencing sleep paralysis, you are conscious while your body is paralyzed and unable to move. For many, feelings of panic and terror come along with sleep paralysis, in addition to the feeling that some evil presence is approaching or choking their body. Sleep paralysis was famously depicted in an oil painting, called *The Nightmare*, done in 1781 by Anglo-Swiss artist Henry Fuseli. The painting shows a demonic figure sitting atop the chest of a woman in deep sleep with her arms outstretched above her. Likewise, in Chinese, the phrase for sleep paralysis is *gui ya shen*, which is loosely translates as "a ghost squeezing the body." In nearly every culture, the concept of sleep paralysis exists, which reinforces the fact that we all dream, no matter what our culture or background. Learning to become more aware of your own consciousness can help ease sleep paralysis. By learning to control their emotions and staying calm, many lucid dreamers can stop sleep paralysis. The best way to counteract the terrifying effects of this phenomenon is to accept your feelings and use the opportunity of consciousness to transition seamlessly into a lucid dream.

TIP TO STOP THE TERRIFYING FEELING OF SLEEP PARALYSIS: Just relax. This may seem counterintuitive, but once you are able to do so, simply visualize becoming lucid. If you really want to exit the sleep paralysis state, try holding your breath until your body awakens.

STRENGTHENING YOUR VOICE

Do you sing? Perhaps you subscribe to the belief that there are people who can sing, and then there are people who cannot sing.

Studies have shown that less than 2 percent of the population is actually tone-deaf, so it follows that most people can actually sing on pitch and hit correct notes—each person just has an unique voice. Singing has been found to be good for the soul and the body. One study of Swedish choir singers found that their heartbeats "synchronize when they sing together," and this results in "a calming effect" that is "as beneficial as yoga." If you've been told that you're not a good singer, or are too shy to karaoke or to even sing in the shower, singing in a lucid dream can be powerfully therapeutic. Most people will be surprised by their incredible singing voice during a lucid dream—usually thanks to a complete lack of inhibition (just as in real life, when you let go of worrying about how you sound, you will likely sing better). Singing in a lucid dream can be a transformative experience, connecting you back to the strength of your voice. Professional songwriters may find inspiration for songwriting, while professional singers may practice their trills and runs freely in a lucid dream as well.

INCREASING YOUR ATHLETIC ABILITY

As an avid climber and yogi, athletics is an important part of my life. I've had a few lucid dreams in which I've practiced a bouldering (a form of rock climbing) problem I had failed to master in real life, only to achieve success in my dream and then go back the next day, in real life, to repeat the simulated success. Athletes of all kinds have used mental rehearsal techniques for years, and lucid dream action actually stimulates the same area of the brain when the action is performed in a waking state. One 2011 study on dream movement by the Max Planck Institute of Psychiatry suggests that performing a task during a lucid dream has a stronger impact on the brain than simple mental rehearsal while awake. Further, a 2000 study conducted by Stephen LaBerge even found that "dreaming consciousness is nearly identical to waking perceptual consciousness, and just as distinct from imagination as imagination is distinct from perception," which implies that lucid dreaming sports practice is just as effective as waking practice—except those who participate in lucid dreaming athletic training gain the advantage of having twice as much time to practice, and that dream mental rehearsal may be even more effective.

PROBLEM-SOLVING

If you're facing a particularly thorny problem in your professional or personal life, lucid dreaming is an incredible tool for problem-solving. In Stephen LaBerge and Howard Rheingold's 1990 book, *Exploring the World of Lucid Dreaming*, they describe a computer programmer who brainstorms with Einstein in his lucid dreams, while working on computer code with him: "I'm sitting with Einstein, white bushy hair . . . he and I are good friends. We do some flowcharts on a blackboard. Once we think we've come up with a good one, we laugh . . . I look at the code and say to myself, 'I want to remember this when I wake up.' I concentrate very hard on the blackboard and wake up . . . I take the code to work and usually it is 99% accurate." One 2012 study of lucid dreamers showed that some of the most frequent applications involved "solving problems (29.9%), getting creative ideas or insights (27.6%) and practicing skills (21.3%)." Any problem of any size can be tackled in a dream. Before going to bed, you can simply visualize the problem at hand, and then focus on it while drifting off to sleep. This will help prompt your subconscious to transform the problem into a dream, and then, when you become lucid, you can work on it even further. Simply having more lucid dreams may just make you a better problem-solver in your waking life as well: A study at the University of Lincoln, England in 2014 found that people with frequent lucid dreams are better at performing cognitive tasks that involve insight, such as problem-solving.

NURTURING CREATIVITY

The dreamscape can be shockingly and beautifully surreal. Salvador Dalí is perhaps one of the most famous lucid dreamers in the art world. His paintings are full of otherworldly imagery, such as elephants walking on impossibly long and thin legs like stilts (*Temptation of Saint Anthony*), the infamous melting clocks (*The Persistence of Memory*), and two roaring tigers, jumping out of a goldfish's gaping mouth that is emerging out of a pomegranate (*Dream Caused by the Flight of a Bee around a Pomegranate a Second before Awakening*). His technique for capturing the fantastical images produced by his brain during sleep was to place a tin plate on the floor beneath him, next to his seated position on a chair. Dalí would hold a spoon over the plate, and then begin to relax into the dream state. As soon as he dozed off, the spoon would slip from his grip and land with a clattering noise on the plate below, which would awaken him back to reality with the dream images still fresh in his mind, ready to be captured. As a writer, I've also had dreams in which I've been able to meet my fictional characters while asleep, and talk to them. No matter which creative medium you pursue, the dreamscape is a blank slate, just waiting for your experimentation. You could sculpt people out of clay, paint the sky with your fingers, create a beat by tapping flower petals . . . the possibilities are endless, and yours for the taking. The works of art that you create in your dreams are simply prototypes for creation in the waking world. As Pablo Picasso famously said, "Everything you can dream is real."

HEALING PAST TRAUMA

Growing up in central New Jersey with immigrant parents from Taiwan, my family and I faced a lot of racism. We were shunned by a majority of our neighbors in subtle, yet vicious ways. Even though I've moved on with my life and am very happy, for a long time, part of me still held a grudge against those people who didn't know any better. In one recurring dream I had in my late twenties, I found myself in my childhood neighborhood, and face-to-face with one particularly insidious woman who was a huge gossip. As

I became lucid, I finally confronted her and yelled at her loudly, calling her out for all the racist things she'd said. I pointed out how her actions had been childlike and hurtful. When I awoke, I felt as if a burden had been lifted off my shoulders. Since it had been years since I'd seen that woman, and because my parents no longer live in that neighborhood, there was little chance I'd ever have the chance to confront my past in the real world. The idea of reenacting past trauma in order to heal was actually studied in 2016 by a researcher named Dr. Gerlinde Harb, who worked with thirty-three Iraq and Afghanistan combat veterans to examine the possible healing effect lucid dreaming could have on their PTSD. The patients were taught image rehearsal therapy, which allowed them to control their dream content more and relieve stress from recurring nightmares, resulting in a significant improvement with this type of treatment.

HEALING THE PHYSICAL BODY

While the Greeks used sleeping temples to incubate cures for their physical ailments, some lucid dreamers today are taking healing matters into their own dream hands. Lucidity researchers Ed Kellogg and Robert Waggoner have investigated the possibility of using lucid dreaming to actually heal the physical body. In 1989, Dr. Kellogg used lucid dreaming to heal an infected tonsil, with remarkable results that showed "dramatic improvement." Later, at the 2007 PsiberDreaming Conference, Kellogg presented a workshop called "Mind-Body Healing through Dreamwork," in which participants looked at three different types of healing dreams: (1) diagnostic healing dreams, which call attention to health problems the dreamer has that may have gone undetected or diagnosed; (2) prescriptive healing dreams, in which a lucid dreamer asks in his dream for foods to eat to cure his illness or other actions to speed his healing, and (3) curative healing dreams, in which a lucid dreamer cures her conditions entirely, such as one woman who reportedly imagined a healing ball of white light on her plantar warts in a dream; she woke up to find that they'd turned black and fallen off in her sleep.

There have been other reports of successful uses of lucid dreaming to prompt overnight disappearances of inflammation, due to chronic bursitis; the elimination of a herpes sore; and the elimination of a chronic (over twenty years) case of bronchitis. Writer and lucid dream teacher Charlie Morley has also self-reported that he's healed ear infections and torn ligaments through lucid dream visualizations. Later on, in chapter 8, we'll explore the possibilities of lucid dream healing in greater depth.

FREEDOM OF MOVEMENT

For anyone who has a limited range of motion in waking life—like those who are paralyzed, injured, disabled, ill, elderly, or are otherwise restricted in their movement—lucid dreaming can give the dreamer the experience of moving within a fully functional dream body. For the injured, in much the way that lucid dreams of practicing a sport can help improve an athlete's game, lucid dreams of physical therapy can help speed recovery and rehabilitation. Lucid dreaming can be an excellent means of exploring the world freely and without any bodily restrictions during sleep.

BECOMING ANOTHER PERSON

Perhaps you want to have more empathy, or perhaps you're a writer or actor and you'd like to do an in-depth character study. Changing your identity in a lucid dream can allow you to feel what it is like to be a lazy cat lying in the sun on a porch, or to be a butterfly floating in the wind, or to be a small child again or an elderly person on the brink of death, or to be a person with a background and personal history completely foreign to your own. If everyone were able to physically embody other people—to truly feel what it is like to be in somebody else's shoes—there would be a lot more empathy in this world, and perhaps more understanding that we are all connected, and human.

PSYCHEDELIC EXPERIENCE

If you've ever had a hallucinogenic experience, you may have experienced what a lucid dream feels like. Reality becomes at once sharper and more vivid. Psychedelic states can induce visual patterns in everything, or the sensation that reality feels like a dream. Depending on where you live, psychedelics such as LSD (lysergic acid diethylamide, also known as "acid") and psilocybin may be illegal. While mind-altering substances like alcohol are completely legal and socially acceptable, psychedelics have been criminalized, vilified, and regarded as dangerous, even though they may be quite useful in terms of healing. Thanks to the work of organizations like the Multidisciplinary Association for Psychedelic Studies (MAPS), founded in 1986, substances like magic mushrooms and LSD have become decriminalized for use in research, and their studies show a correlation between usage of these drugs and overcoming addiction and trauma. But to fast-track yourself into a trippy psychedelic state without the risk of breaking the law or other real-world consequences, you can simply lucid dream.

Finding Your Lucid Dreaming Intention

Why do you want to lucid dream? Intention is everything, so before you embark on a lucid dream journey, you may want to list your reasons for pursuing lucid dreaming. This will give you even more clarity on your purpose, which will help you achieve your lucidity goals. For obvious reasons, one of the first steps toward lucid dreaming is to remember your dreams. If you currently don't recall your dreams upon waking, the best way to do so is to start paying attention to your dreams (more on how to remember your dreams in the next chapter). What unresolved issues do you have? What problems do you have that you may be neglecting? What are your dream patterns? What keeps you up at night? Which of these avenues do you want to explore first? Writing or outlining a map to your lucidity goals is a task that can help clarify what you want and solidify the plan to achieve it, which will then pop up in your subconscious at night.

❖ 4 ❖

LAYING THE FOUNDATIONS FOR A LUCID DREAM

"If the dream is a translation of waking life, waking life is also a translation of the dream."

—RENÉ MAGRITTE

RENÉ MAGRITTE WAS A FAMOUS BELGIAN PAINTER, known for his surrealist works, such as *Man with a Bowler Hat* (1964), and his depictions of visually impossible scenes, such as *Empire of Light* (1950), in which the façade of a house at night in the foreground is juxtaposed against a bright blue, sunlit sky in the background. His art is rooted in a suspension of disbelief in which accepted laws of "reality" and what is possible are put on hold. To be a lucid dreamer is to similarly suspend our disbelief and limitations, to have an open mind and to believe in our imagination as the dominant force in our universe.

There are many ways to start training yourself to lucid dream, but the best advice I've ever heard is to simply believe that you can and will. This belief—paired with absolute, focused attention—is the most effective path to lucid dreaming. Training the mind and teaching yourself to maintain attentiveness are key to lucid dreaming, because once you can cultivate a constant awareness throughout your waking day, you will be able to carry that state over into the dream world. And while there are many tips, tricks, hacks, herbal supplements, and fancy lucid dreaming masks out on the market to help you manipulate your dreams, none of these lucidity aids are helpful if you can't remember your dreams. The first step to lucidity is to build a strong foundation of dream recall.

REMEMBERING YOUR DREAMS

If you never remember your dreams, the first thing you must do is stop identifying yourself as such. To echo the famous therapist Marisa Peer, the body really listens to the words you use, and takes them to heart. If you say that you have a bad memory or never remember your dreams, you'll likely not remember your dreams. So, moving forward, tell yourself that you will remember your dreams, and that, in fact, you have an excellent dream memory. It's possible that you don't remember your dreams because you've simply never paid attention to or thought about them. I've had many conversations with friends and acquaintances about lucid dreaming, only for them to text me with excitement a few days later that they remembered their dreams, just because we had discussed the topic.

Another way to prepare your mind and body for excellent dream recall is to have a regular sleep schedule and to exercise—an added benefit of pursuing lucid dreaming is that, generally, it promotes a healthy overall lifestyle. Setting an alarm to wake up early is another good way to catch your consciousness mid-dream, since REM cycles often occur early, that is, before sunrise. But setting an alarm doesn't mean you have to get up right away. When you awaken, try to remain as still as possible, since moving around or starting your regular morning routine will trigger your mind to think about the day ahead and a train of thoughts, worries, and to-dos may follow.

As soon as you're awake, don't move; instead, simply review any details of the dream you just had. When you have a firm grasp on the dream narrative, you can then reach for a pen and a dream journal or an audio recording device to capture the dream. Alternatively, if you're still tired afterward, you can allow yourself to drift back to sleep, holding the intention in mind to remember any dreams you might have.

STEP 1 TO REMEMBERING YOUR DREAMS:
Tell yourself before going to bed that you will remember your dream.

BEDTIME RITUALS, NOT ROUTINES

Establishing a sleep routine is important, but it may be more powerful to establish a ritual. While a routine and ritual both involve repeated acts, the main difference between them is that a ritual is imbued with meaning. Our minds are highly suggestible, and even more so right before going to bed. If you've found yourself without an alarm clock and told your brain that you had to wake up at a certain time the next day, chances are you'll wake up right on time. The next time you're about to drift off to sleep, tell yourself: *I will remember my dream tonight.* Repeat this in your mind until you fall asleep. Other rituals you can perform before bed might include taking a relaxing bath with salts or essential oils; meditating by candlelight; or placing a particular stone, crystal, or other personally meaningful object underneath your pillow. You could also listen to calming music or a lucid dreaming meditation on YouTube before bed (the best way to do this is to use a speaker and leave the screen out of your bedroom, if possible). You can even write your intentions for dreaming in your dream journal before drifting off to sleep.

A Note on Technology

It's good practice to ban all technology and screens from the bedroom as well. Some people with sensitivity to EMFs (electromagnetic fields) given off by WiFi routers may even find their sleep disturbed because EMFs can cause a reduction in melatonin. So it may be a good idea to shut off the WiFi, too. Unfortunately, as technology has become integrated so deeply into the fabric of everyday life—how we bank, how we socialize, how we work, how we date, how we order goods, how we store memories and, most sadly, how we validate ourselves and find self-worth—many of us spend a shocking amount of time looking at our cell phones. The average American spends more than four and a half hours a day on a cell phone. If you're always looking at your phone, whether it's for "important" work emails or frivolous social media feeds, you're sending your brain the message that whatever is on your screen is of great importance—whether it's targeted advertising or a project for work that is due next week.

DISCONNECTING TO CONNECT TO YOURSELF

To break your own dependency (if any) on technology, I advise banning cell phone usage for at least one hour before going to bed and for at least one hour after waking up. This way, you can allow yourself to focus on your own thoughts, desires, and dreams, before letting the endless stream of other people's posts, work, and advertisements batter your brain. We live in an attention-driven economy, where tech giants want our constant attention to feed their profits. And since so much about learning dream control is learning to control our attention and focus, this will be far easier to do once we conquer the battle against companies who want nothing more than to capitalize on us by making their dreams our own.

STEP 2 TO REMEMBERING YOUR DREAMS:
Have a regular sleep schedule, exercise, and set an alarm
to wake up early to record your dreams. Banish technology
from the bedroom.

DREAM RECORDING

Another surefire tool to boost your dream recall is to keep a dream journal. If you don't have a dream journal yet, grab a notebook and pen, and place them on your nightstand, or an audio recording device if you prefer to speak your dreams. As soon as you wake up in the morning, keep very still and don't move—this will help you stay in the dream world, and have access to your dream memory. When you feel ready, you can grab your recording tools and start scribbling, sketching, or speaking your dream. I've found that it's helpful for dream recall to write or record the dream in the present tense, as if it were happening right now and you were still inside the dream. It's also important to note what emotions you were feeling during the dream. When recording your dream, don't worry about getting everything exactly correct or in chronological order. Just write down any images, phrases, or bits of action you can remember from your dream, since even the act of writing one part can trigger a whole other memory or part of your dream that you had forgotten.

After you've recorded your dream, going back and giving your dream a title will help you synthesize it. Note a few key words, such as where the dream took place, if any important people were in the dream, or any themes.

> **STEP 3 TO REMEMBERING YOUR DREAMS:**
> **Create a written or recorded dream log of all of your dreams, and collect at least a few weeks of data about the content of your dreams.**

ANALYZING YOUR DREAM LOG

After a few weeks, you'll have your own personal dream data log—a gold mine of self-reflection! From there, you can get a sense of over-arching patterns and any recurring subjects or places. Identify a few dreamscapes that recur again and again, and especially places where you keep finding yourself that you no longer have access to in normal life, or people you no longer talk to. For example, if you keep dreaming about being in high school or that you're roaming around your college campus, even though you graduated years ago, that's a clear dream pattern. Or, if you are talking to your deceased grandma or find yourself flying—anything that would never happen in everyday life, take note of it.

DESIGNATING YOUR DREAM SIGNS

Once you've taken inventory of all your dreams, you can make a list of your recurring dream signs and patterns. Pick the top five to ten recurring dream scenes, write them in a permanent marker, and post them somewhere visible:

IF I AM _____, THEN I AM DREAMING.

Post these around your house, on your phone, at your work desk—this will ensure that the next time you find yourself in one of those situations, you'll be triggered to recognize that you're in a dream.

> **STEP 4 TO REMEMBERING YOUR DREAMS:**
> **Analyze your dream log and identify the top five common dream themes. Then create sticky note reminders around your home, work, or car to remind you to check if you are dreaming throughout the day.**

LIFESTYLE FACTORS

Lifestyle choices can have an impact on dream recall. Smoking cigarettes or ingesting marijuana, for example, suppresses REM cycle activity during sleep; therefore, users actually dream less. One upside, though, is that if you stop smoking, it may trigger intense REM cycles. Regular weed users have anecdotally reported that if they stop smoking marijuana, a flurry of vivid dreams comes rushing to their consciousness on mornings when they awaken. Other illegal drugs, such as cocaine and ecstasy (aka MDMA), negatively impact sleep quality and repress REM cycles, causing fewer dreams. Conversely, while alcohol (which is a highly popular and legal substance) also negatively impacts the quality of one's sleep, it causes a more shallow sleep and *more* REM cycles—but getting drunk is not a wise path to lucidity. After all, becoming inebriated during our waking lives often causes us to lose clarity and the capacity for good judgment, which is the exact opposite of lucidity. For morning people or caffeine fiends, take note of your daily coffee intake. One study showed that certain amounts of coffee and other caffeinated drinks also caused REM cycles to shift to the earlier part of the night, which may make dream recall more difficult. Green tea is a good (and healthy) coffee alternative that won't impact your REM cycles.

Folklore tells us that eating Stilton cheese before bed causes strange and vivid dreams, and the herb mugwort (ingested via tea or smoked) has been used by Native Americans as a "dream sage" for thousands of years. But a recent 2018 study showed that foods rich in vitamin B6, such as fish, potatoes, and bananas, were effective in helping dreamers remember their nocturnal escapades after waking. However, the best path forward to lucidity is being healthy overall. Another study from 2013 found that a varied diet, which implies a healthier diet, also led to healthier sleep patterns and better dream recall.

PHARMACEUTICALS

Legal drugs—that is, those prescribed by doctors—can also have an impact on sleep and dream recall. Nearly one in two Americans take prescription drugs, all with varying effects on dreams and dream recall. People who are attempting to quit smoking with a nicotine patch have reported an increase in vivid and intense dreams. Some treatments for Alzheimer's disease (donepezil, rivastigmine, galantamine, and memantine) have also been associated with reports of increased dream recall, more vivid dreaming, and even more lucid dreams. Sadly, more often than not, pharmaceutical drugs merely treat symptoms, rather than addressing the problem. Interestingly, the sleeping aid pill Ambien has reported side effects of hypnosis, amnesia, and hallucinations—some people have even reported experiences as bizarre as out-of-body floating and having folded their laundry during their sleep without even realizing it. To fully achieve lucidity, it may be helpful to revisit your medicine cabinet and consult with your doctor to determine which drugs you've been prescribed are absolutely necessary.

STEP 5 TO REMEMBERING YOUR DREAMS:

Do an audit of your overall lifestyle. Are you healthy? Are you exercising? What kind of foods are you eating and which drugs are your preferred poison? Developing a healthier lifestyle will have the dual benefit of generally enhancing your life and inducing lucidity.

❖ 5 ❖

WAYS TO LUCIDITY

"Be careful what you water your dreams with.
Water them with worry and fear and you will produce weeds
that choke the life from your dream. Water them with optimism
and solutions and you will cultivate success."

—LAO TZU

YOU'VE CREATED A SOLID FOUNDATION OF good sleeping habits and have started a dream journal. At this point, having a lucid dream can be as easy for some as identifying key dream patterns and then learning to recognize them in a familiar dream environment. For others, lucidity will happen by incorporating reality checks into daily life, which will then carry over into dream life. Some may prefer more direct lucid dreaming induction, for which there are various methods and tricks you can practice, according to your own schedule. But, no matter how you gain lucidity, it's important to remember that everyone is capable of becoming lucid. No matter what your belief system, it's important to *believe that it is possible to become lucid*.

Try out the following techniques to induce lucidity, and don't be afraid to experiment with what works best for you. Once you become lucid for the first time, it can also trigger an incredibly exciting rush and flood of excitement. But, remember, staying calm is important! We'll dive deeper into how to maintain and extend lucidity later on. First things first: You have to ask yourself a key question, and it's important to take this next question very seriously.

Are you dreaming right now?

REALITY CHECKS

Did you check if you were dreaming? How could you tell? How can you tell if you're in a dream? Perhaps you didn't even stop to check, because you assumed that you were reading, so, of course, you are awake. But you can read in dreams, too, and given the fact that nobody really knows the true nature of reality, it's hard to prove that none of us are dreaming right now.

We are all so used to accepting everything that we see before us, that even in fantastical dreams, it's not a natural inclination for us to stop and question the nature of reality. Are we all in the matrix? Are we all living in a hologram or a computer simulation? One of the most common ways to break into a bout of lucidity is to make a habit out of regular reality checks. The most important aspect of a reality check is that it must be done with actual belief that you *could* be dreaming right now. It sounds like a crazy thing to approach your life with the belief that what you're experiencing right now might be either real or a dream, but it is a prerequisite for becoming lucid. It's about questioning reality, without accepting the circumstances as they are, and carrying on. The concept of reality checks is to make them a habit that you will carry through to your dream world. Then when you do a reality check in the dream world, it'll trigger this grand realization: Life is but a dream.

Here are a few common reality checks to carry out through the day:

HAND CHECK: Throughout the day, take a good look at your hands. Oftentimes in dreams, people will see that their hands have fewer or more than the usual five digits.

LIGHT SWITCH: Oftentimes in dreams, if you attempt to turn a light switch on or off, it doesn't work. When you enter or leave a room, it's a good test to flick the switch up and down to see if it's working properly. If not, it's likely you are dreaming. A word of caution on this one, however: Once, I did the light switch test on a groggy morning in a hotel, and the switch didn't work. For a little while, I incorrectly assumed that I was dreaming before the hotel concierge informed me that the lights were broken.

BREATHING TEST: Your dream body, unlike your real-life waking body, does not need oxygen to operate. One solid reality test is to pinch your nose with your mouth closed and to try to inhale sharply. If you can continue to do this without any problems or shortness of breath, you're likely in a dream. It's a very discreet way to check throughout the day if you are dreaming.

JUMP TO FLIGHT TEST: If you suspect that you're in a dream, a good way to confirm that is to jump up or to attempt to fly. The moment your feet leave the floor without returning, you can be sure that you're in a dream. For more active lucid dreamers, a good way to test reality throughout the day is to jump up and down at every coffee break. Remember, actually expecting to be able to float will cause you to do so in a dream, and then confirm the state.

DOUBLE TAKE ON WORDS AND TIMEPIECES: In dreams, words are very unstable. I make it a habit to read a sign, then look away, and then look back quickly again to see if the arrangement of letters has sneakily changed. Usually, the words will change in a dream, which can be a sure sign (literally) that you are sleeping. Once I found myself in a dream, writing words on a chalkboard. The words kept becoming misspelled, which frustrated me, until I realized that I was dreaming! Another popular reality check is to look once at your wristwatch or any clock to verify the time. Look away, and then if you look back only to find that the time has suddenly changed—you're dreaming.

MIRROR METHOD: Most dream mirrors are trick mirrors, so it's always a good reality check to take a long look in the mirror and to study your reflection carefully. One way to incorporate frequent reality checks this way is to look in the mirror every time you go to the bathroom. In the dream world, your reflection may show something other than what you'd expect. Mirrors can also act as portals in lucid dreams, so if you do happen to find yourself dreaming, try to climb through the mirror and see where it takes you.

HAVE A TOTEM: Like the spinning top in *Inception*, you can choose a small object to carry around with you to check whether or not you're dreaming. The key to having a totem work is to attach special significance to it, and, as with any reality check, you must take it seriously. Keep your totem on you at all times—you can use a poker chip, a die, or any small charm or tchotchke that you wish. Then, assign a dream action to your totem item—it can be that when you toss the die, it'll float in the air, or a fidget spinner that works on its own when dropped, or a special pen that writes in sparkly pink glitter in the air. When you use the item in everyday life and nothing happens, you can assume you're not dreaming. If magic ensues, then you're ready for dream action. But the trick is to believe that, in a dream, the dream action associated with the item will happen.

RETRACE YOUR MEMORY: How did you get here, to this point, right now? Can you retrace your steps of the day leading up to this very moment? If you suddenly jumped from the deck of a cruise ship to a ski lift, or made any other seemingly impossible leap or sudden switch of environment, you're likely dreaming. This also doubles as a fun awareness exercise to employ throughout your day.

TIME CHECK: Get a wristwatch or another timer to beep every hour. This is a great way to ensure that reality checks will become a constant habit that will carry over to the dream world. Again, it is important to take the reality check seriously and to give it your full attention each time—otherwise, you run the risk of unconsciously doing reality checks in a blasé manner, which will result in missing serious cues that you are dreaming.

THE STRANGER TEST: As an extrovert, one of my favorite reality checks is to ask complete strangers if I'm dreaming, and then do another reality check as a backup. If I'm stopping somewhere to get coffee, I'll ask the barista, "Am I dreaming right now?" The backup reality check is essential here, because dream characters can have strange responses to this question, depending on your own subconscious. But even if you use this method and you're not dreaming, I've found that it often sparks an interesting conversation with a stranger, and generally raises awareness about dreams in our communities and in society.

THE POWER OF AWARENESS

All these reality checks are meant to cultivate one thing—awareness. Unfortunately, modern life requires most of us to submit to a repetitive routine that we fall into without questioning. Most people wake up, check their phone, brush their teeth, and do the same exact things on autopilot mode. Or they eat lunch and have conversations in a distracted state, reliving angry moments of the past, ruminating over regrets, or they worry anxiously about the future. When your mind is not present, it's nearly impossible to pay attention to your surroundings and to your reality, which is why most people never question the nature of reality in dreams, even when what's happening is completely fantastical, or logic and the laws of gravity are being openly defied.

❊ ❊ ❊ ❊ ❊ ❊ ❊ ❊ ❊ ❊ ❊ ❊ ❊

REVIEW THE DAY BACKWARD:
An Exercise to Build Awareness

If you're looking for a great way to build your awareness and focus, one exercise recommended by author Neville Goddard is to review your day before going to bed. As you lie in bed, go through every action you took that day, starting with the most recent and working backward. So if you are in bed, imagine the steps you took to get there—you just turned off the light, and before that you brushed your teeth, washed your face, changed into pajamas, took a shower, and so on, until you've reached the moment when you woke up. By practicing this exercise, you'll be able to strengthen your focus and attention tremendously, and it also has the added benefit of bringing your awareness to everything you did that day.

❊ ❊ ❊ ❊ ❊ ❊ ❊ ❊ ❊ ❊ ❊ ❊ ❊

THE RULES OF REALITY (CHECKS)

Another important note on reality checks is that none of these are hard-and-fast rules. The dream world doesn't seem to have absolute laws that govern it. For example, when I first started lucid dreaming, I would check my hands to do a reality check and would always see seven or eight fingers on a hand. I had read somewhere that, in a dream, you never have five fingers—always fewer or more. But later on, as I started lucid dreaming more and more often, I would look at my hands and see that both had five fingers, just as in everyday life. I would then perform another reality check, but had cultivated enough awareness to know that I was dreaming. Another popular myth was that, in a lucid dream, you can't say your own name without waking up, which has been disproved by other lucid dreamers. The takeaway here is to be wary of any dogmatic rules of what is and is not possible, and their impact on how you live your dreams (and your waking life). As Henry Ford famously said, "Believe that you can, or believe that you can't—either way, you're right."

DIRECT INDUCTION METHODS TO LUCIDITY

Sometimes, merely creating a regular sleep routine, increasing dream recall, keeping a dream journal, and integrating daily reality checks into your life can be enough to trigger lucidity. However, if you find yourself wanting to take more direct action to induce lucidity, or you simply want to increase the number of your lucid dreams, there are a variety of induction methods you can use.

The DILD (Dream-Induced Lucid Dream) Method

One of the simplest ways to induce a lucid dream is just to recognize that you're dreaming as it's happening. During a dream-induced lucid dream, you gain lucidity within the dream itself—this is where all the preparation work you've done for lucid dreaming comes into play. By recognizing your common dream signs or by performing a habitual reality check while you're dreaming, you'll be well-prepared to become aware that you're dreaming. Oftentimes, people will report that they've been using the DILD method their entire lives, because they were natural-born lucid dreamers.

The MILD (Mnemonic-Induced Lucid Dream) Method

The MILD (Mnemonic-Induced Lucid Dream) technique was pioneered by Dr. Stephen LaBerge. After LaBerge started using this method, the number of lucid dreams he had per month drastically increased—from one per month to as many as four per night. This method simply relies on intent to lucid dream and remembering that intent. It also relies on increasing the strength of our "prospective memory," which is the ability to recall our future intentions without relying on external factors. It's like remembering a list of things to buy at a grocery store without the list you made in front of you. With the MILD technique, you're essentially training your brain to associate certain things with remembering to check if you're dreaming—your dream signs, but also mundane things like walking through a doorway or recognizing when a dog barks. But, again, the MILD technique is about intent and seeding your brain with the idea that you will recognize that you're dreaming.

Here's how to perform the MILD technique:

1. **ESTABLISH DREAM RECALL.** Before going to bed each night, make sure to tell yourself that you will remember your dream in the morning.

2. **WAKE UP AND RECALL YOUR DREAM.** Wake up a bit earlier than your normal time, and keep your dream fresh in your mind. Review the details of what happened in your dream over and over again.

3. **FALL BACK ASLEEP WITH *FOCUSED* INTENT.** As you go back to sleep, repeat your intent to remember that you are dreaming inside a dream. Any phrase or mantra helps, like "The next time I am dreaming, I will remember that I am dreaming," or "I will remember to have a lucid dream when I fall asleep." I like to repeat the phrase "I am lucid dreaming" as I drift off to sleep.

4. **IMAGINE YOURSELF LUCID.** As you recall your dream from earlier that morning, imagine being inside the dream. Focus on any dream signs or weird dream details, and tell yourself that you are dreaming.

5. **REPEAT STEPS 3 AND 4 UNTIL LUCIDITY OCCURS.**

The WILD (Wake-Initiated Lucid Dream) Method

Another method pioneered by Dr. LaBerge, the WILD method essentially consists of *staying conscious while your physical body falls asleep*. This means that you remain alert through hypnagogia—the transitional state from wakefulness to sleep. It's a pretty strange experience, because reality becomes warped. Usually, with your eyes closed, you see spots or geometric patterns, or even have hallucinations. Thoughts become untethered, and perhaps nonsensical, as in a dream. But unlike in dreams, one 2013 study found that hypnagogic hallucinations are experienced more from the passive point of view, rather than the immersive point of view. From personal experience, staying conscious while falling asleep is a bizarre experience; it feels as if you're getting sucked through a tunnel into another dimension. I've found that by using the WILD method and focusing calmly on the hypnagogic imagery, it's possible to enter a dream tranquilly.

Here's how to perform the WILD technique:

1. **RELAX YOUR BODY.** This method works best when you've just woken up and are still very relaxed. But if you're more alert, focus on letting go of all the tension in your muscles and on taking deep breaths. Let your mind relax and your thoughts still—if your thoughts continue to buzz, let them carry on without following them until you're completely concentrated on your breathing and having your body supported by your bed.

2. **OBSERVE WITH EYES CLOSED.** With your eyes closed, calmly observe any visual imagery that may appear. It's important to watch as an impartial observer, even as the images develop into more complex scenes. Gradually, these series of disconnected scenes will connect to each other, creating an extended scenario.

3. **PASSIVELY ENTER THE DREAM STATE.** When the scene before you becomes more vivid, resist the temptation to actively enter the dream; this can cause the scene before you to crumble. Instead, allow the dream to progress on its own, without interference. Once you are fully in the dream, beware of forgetting that you are dreaming, because it could be easy to slip back into a non-lucid dream state.

The FILD (Finger-Induced Lucid Dream) Method

For this "fast-track" method to work, you have to be exceedingly tired—perhaps you had a long day of physical exercise, or you slept in late and are in a groggy state, or you woke up in the middle of the night. It's a variation of the WILD technique, except you're using your fingers to keep yourself conscious while you fall asleep. Many claim that this method will get you into a lucid dream extremely quickly.

Here's how the FILD method works:

1. **FIRST, PRACTICE GENTLY MOVING YOUR INDEX AND MIDDLE FINGERS**. Pretend that you're playing a piano or typing different letters on a computer keyboard, one after the other. Don't push down hard, just gently enough to move either the piano key or the letter key.

2. **WHEN YOU'RE REALLY TIRED, RELAX YOUR BODY AND POSITION YOUR HAND ON A FLAT SURFACE**. Now that you've practiced the finger-tapping motion, slowly and gently tap your index and middle fingers, alternating between the two until your body drifts off to sleep.

3. **IN ABOUT THIRTY SECONDS, DO A PALM REALITY CHECK.** If you did everything correctly, you should have slid into a dream. You can stop tapping your fingers and instead perform a reality check to ensure that you're in the dream— and go from there!

Wake Back to Bed Method

Both the MILD and the WILD techniques can be used in conjunction with the Wake Back to Bed method, which entails setting your alarm clock for a few hours earlier than you usually do. Many lucid dreamers report that this technique works the best for inducing lucidity, and it's fairly simple to do. It works well because REM cycles occur more frequently during the later hours of sleep, so by waking up and then going back to sleep right before the high frequency of REM cycles, you can consciously prep your mind to become lucid at this point.

Here's how the Wake Back to Bed Method works:

1. **SET AN ALARM FOR TWO TO THREE HOURS BEFORE YOUR USUAL WAKE-UP TIME.** I've found that this method works well if you stay up a bit later than usual, around midnight or even one in the morning (as long as you have a flexible of schedule during the week; if not, do this on the weekend).

2. **WAKE UP EARLY AND GET OUT OF BED FOR AT LEAST ONE HOUR.** After you record any dream (if you have any), it's important to get out of bed and become fully alert. If you go to sleep around half past midnight, try waking up at 7 a.m. Then, drink some green tea, read your emails, or, better yet, read about lucid dreaming or journal about your lucid dreaming goals.

3. **GO BACK TO BED AND RELAX.** After a few hours of wakefulness, go back to bed and relax your entire body. For at least thirty minutes before falling asleep, focus solely on having a lucid dream, by using either the MILD or WILD method.

HERBAL SUPPLEMENTS VERSUS HERBAL FOLK MAGIC

Mugwort is a popular herb used to help trigger lucidity, and it is one of the main ingredients in a lucid dreaming supplement called Dream Leaf. The company's marketing tactics are clever: The red and blue pills (which are a direct nod to the pills Neo is forced to choose between in *The Matrix*) are touted as "the most advanced lucid dreaming supplement on the market," and claim to help improve dream recall, promote balanced sleep, and lengthen REM cycles, in addition to triggering lucidity. Whether these expensive pills work or if the placebo effect is at play here is debatable, but according to author Jared Zeizel, who wrote *A Field Guide to Lucid Dreaming: Mastering the Art of Oneironautics*, there "aren't any short-cuts to having a lucid dream." But to be fair to these overpriced and well-marketed gimmick pills, mugwort does have other beneficial properties for health in general. It can aid digestion, reduce anxiety, and promote relaxation, so it can't hurt anything except your wallet to try out these pills.

Moreover, there may be something to using plants intentionally to help you cultivate your ability to lucid dream.

One of my anthropologist and writer friends, Grace Zhou, who is based in California, practices herbal magic to incubate lucid dreams. She studied folk herbalism with Liz Migliorelli, and learned about the power of plants used in dreams, divination, and magic. According to them, the most important baseline before engaging in herbal folk magic is to first cultivate our relationship to these plants and their mythologies. For example, if you're interested in using herbal folk magic as a conduit to the dream world, you may want to sow and tend to your chosen plants in a garden or even a windowsill planter. Read and learn as much as you can about the plants, including their uses and their connotations in folk stories and myth. According to Grace, dreaming with any plant is possible "because they are all conduits between worlds . . . they are living beings who have their roots in the underworld." Nervines—herbs such as lavender, lemon balm, skullcap, blue vervain, milky oat tops, catnip, chamomile, hops, and mugwort—are good for dreaming because they soothe the nervous system and enhance our awareness of our own bodies. And, after all, lucidity is nothing but awareness.

THE *WU WEI* CONCEPT APPLIED TO LUCID DREAMING

If you try all these lucidity techniques and still can't seem to wake up inside a dream, you may want to stop trying. There is a Chinese concept called called *wu wei*, which is literally translated as "inaction," but is loosely translated as "doing nothing" or "strategic nonaction." It's a philosophy that espouses not trying too hard and cultivating a sense of awareness while flowing with the forces of nature around you. If you find yourself frustrated with reality checks or with any of these methods to induce lucidity, the best method may be to simply stop trying for a bit. Just observe your day and your own actions carefully without judgment. Before going to bed, simply tell yourself that you'll be very observant in your dreams, and don't try too hard to achieve lucidity. Oftentimes, when you stop trying so hard, lucidity will occur naturally.

❖ 6 ❖

LIVING THE LUCID DREAM

"Our truest life is when we are in dreams awake."
—HENRY DAVID THOREAU

ONE OF THE FIRST TIMES I EVER BECAME lucid, I was in the middle of climbing through a window of a stone building. Suddenly, it occurred to me that I was dreaming. My heart raced and I couldn't focus on anything other than the fact that I was dreaming. I became so excited that the stone building I was climbing crumbled into pieces, followed by the dream world that I had been in. Before I knew it, I woke up and was back in my bed, gasping for air, heart beating loudly in my chest. I was thrilled that I had become lucid, but every early breakthrough I had inside a dream excited me so much that it sent me back to the waking world. Thanks to the lucid dream pioneers before me,

I then learned a host of techniques to maintain and extend lucidity, which are outlined below.

TIPS TO MAINTAIN AND EXTEND LUCIDITY

Once you've gained lucidity, either through a successful reality check or a wake-initiated lucid dream, it's a landmark moment. But like the first moments of riding a bicycle without training wheels, it's important to remember that it's only the beginning of your lucid journey! Here are some tips while navigating a dream to maintain lucidity, and to extend your lucid dream so that you don't have a premature awakening.

Calm Your Emotions

Since a flood of emotions in lucid dreams disrupts lucidity (especially if the emotion is negative, like frustration or annoyance), it's important to stay calm. Of all of the tips to maintaining lucidity, controlling your own emotions, mind-set, and focus is the most important. A daily meditation practice has been the single best thing for my lucid dreaming practice, because it lays a foundation of awareness. This helps with reality checks, and allows me to control my emotions, and to observe without judging or reacting. From there, dream stabilization and lucidity are the logical next steps.

※ ※ ※ ※ ※ ※ ※ ※ ※ ※ ※ ※

Start a Meditation Practice

If you haven't meditated before, it's extremely easy to start a practice—no in-depth knowledge, apps, or fancy materials required. All it takes is five minutes a day. Here's how to start:

1. **PICK A REGULAR TIME TO MEDITATE.** Mornings or evenings work well—either when you first wake up or when you are about to go to bed. For beginners, meditating for just five minutes can have an incredibly beneficial impact on well-being, focus, and attention.

2. **FIND A COMFORTABLE SPOT TO SIT DOWN.** Try sitting cross-legged with your hands in the mudra position (with the tips of your thumb and index finger touching, forming a circle, and your hands placed on your knees in seated meditation with your palms facing up). Or, if that's too uncomfortable, sit in a chair. Lying down is not recommended, since you can easily fall asleep in this position. Set a timer for five minutes.

3. **EXHALE ALL THE AIR IN YOUR BODY, AND THEN TAKE A DEEP INHALE THROUGH YOUR NOSE.** Exhale again through your mouth, and then gently close your eyes. Continue to inhale and exhale with closed eyes, focusing gently on the breath going through your nostrils and out of your mouth.

4. **CONTINUE TO FOCUS.** If thoughts of the coming day, tasks you have to do, bitter memories of the past, or worries about the future flit through your mind, that's okay. Just observe the thought and then let it pass, returning your focus to your breath. Keep breathing until time is up, and that's it!

❀ ❀ ❀ ❀ ❀ ❀ ❀ ❀ ❀ ❀ ❀ ❀

Pay Attention to Your Body

If you've already looked at your hands for a reality check, you may want to examine them further. Try rubbing your hands together, and then continue to observe your dream body—not just your hands, but your arms, your legs, your stomach. Focus on each movement and become aware of your dream body, as you might do in a yoga class. This will focus your attention on your dream body and help stabilize yourself so you can stay in the dream.

Spinning Technique

First invented by Dr. Stephen LaBerge, the spinning technique consists of simply spinning your body around as soon as you notice your dream beginning to fade. Oftentimes, when the dream begins to lose color and detail and realism, that means it's ending. To prevent this, simply stretch out your arms and start to spin in circles, like a top. Focus on your dream body in motion, and concentrate on recognizing that when you stop, you'll see a dream scene before your eyes. Because the sensations of movement in the dream feel as real as actually moving, LaBerge hypothesizes that this technique is so effective because spinning stimulates "the system of the brain that integrates vestibular activity detected in the middle ear, [which] facilitates the activity of the nearby components of the REM sleep system." This vestibular system may be involved with the "production of rapid eye movement bursts in REM sleep." Thus, if you focus on spinning, it may just keep you in a REM cycle.

Put on Glasses

If the dream scene before you becomes blurry or loses its vividness, you may find it helpful to imagine a pair of glasses. This is a nifty psychological trick that uses a dream prop (I have done this by simply reaching into my pocket and expecting to find a pair of glasses) to help you maintain lucidity in a dream.

Listen to External Voices or Noises

If people are speaking in your dream, or if you hear any external noises, such as music or trucks driving by in the background, try to home in on those noises. Focusing on any external sounds can help ground you in the dream and stabilize the entire scene.

Demand Clarity

Another method to stabilize a dream and to regain clarity in a lucid dream is to use your own dream voice and demand it. To do so, just say to yourself out loud that you are dreaming. You can even request clarity from your own subconscious. Use any phrase you'd like, but short and simple commands, like "I am dreaming" or "Clarity, please," work best. Oftentimes, by using your own voice and force of will, the dream will begin to stabilize and you'll become even more lucid, allowing you to continue forward in the lucid state.

Touch Objects

Like listening to external voices or noise in a dream, it's very helpful to pick up and focus on the tactile feeling of any object that may be near you—a chair, a book, anything. Again, be sure to really home in on the texture of what you're holding. Feel its weight, size, and shape in your hands to help stabilize the dream. It also helps to rub your hands together before doing so.

Do a Math Problem

German researcher Paul Tholey discovered that doing math in dreams requires far more mental concentration than in waking life. Thus, by doing simple mental math in a dream, such as adding 2 + 2, you'll activate the conscious brain and increase your mental alertness, which will also help stabilize the dream. Just be sure to keep the math problem simple (no calculus, unless you're a mathematician), or else you may lose yourself in solving the problem and then also lose lucidity.

Start Flying

One great way to keep a lucid dream stable as soon as you've achieved lucidity is also one of the most rewarding—start flying. To do so, you can simply jump up in the air, or start running and take off. This act forces you to concentrate heavily on your dream body, and also gives you the sensation of being in motion, as spinning does. It has the added benefit of taking you to a new place, and you can watch the dream scene evolve before your eyes.

If You're Awake, Play Dead

If you do happen to wake up from your dream, the best course of action is not to take any. Don't move; just stay calm and relaxed, because you're in the best position, physically and mentally, to return to a lucid dream. Keep your eyes closed and simply focus on the last scene you had in your mind until you find yourself back in the same dream.

INCREASE YOUR LUCID DREAMING CONTROL

Now that you've mastered stabilizing your dreams and maintaining lucidity, the next step is to augment your lucid dreaming control abilities. When I first began lucid dreaming, I found that whenever I was flying, it was difficult to control my flight pattern, as if I were flying a plane and couldn't quite manage the controls. But slowly, with the following lucid dreaming workshop tools, I was able to build up my level of lucid dream control.

Ask for Help

In one of my first lucid dreams ever, I remember being in a wide-open field, and, in the distance, there was an incredible sunset that had turned the sky a deep orange, blended into a creamy yellow. I did not want the sun to set yet, and, since I was lucid, I realized that because it was my dream, the sun did not have to set. But I didn't know how to move the sun back up in the sky yet. Suddenly, I saw a young guy in his early twenties, who was dressed all in black, like a production assistant on a film set (I had worked on a few film sets at the time). I went up to him, and I asked him if he knew how I could move the sun back higher up in the sky. "Oh, yeah sure," he responded. "You just go like this," and he took his finger and pointed it at the sun, and then moved it up slowly. I then tried it myself by taking my own index finger, pointing it at the sun, and flicking it with my finger even higher in the sky. Suddenly, it was noon, the sky was blue, and neither of us had shadows. I thanked him and went on my way.

Talk to Dream Characters

Beyond asking for help, talk to your dream characters if you're looking for any sort of advice in gaining lucidity. In another dream I had, I found myself on what appeared to be a tour bus in a beautiful city in Spain. Gaining lucidity on the bus, I suddenly turned to one of my dream characters, an older blond woman, who was dressed like she was from the Midwest. "I'm dreaming!" I announced to her, only to get a response that baffled me. "I know," she said calmly, "I am, too. Lucid dreaming is a cheap way to travel, since I don't have much money!" It's still unclear whether or not shared dreaming is possible— that is, if it is possible to meet another conscious being in a dream. But, either way, engaging in conversations with your dream characters is an excellent way to learn more about your dream and about yourself.

Tinker with a Dream Television (Or a Virtual AI Device)

This technique was pioneered by expert lucid dreamer Alan Worsley (who, you may recall, was the subject of the famous eye-movement test that proved the existence of lucid dreaming); it involves tinkering with a television set. When lucid, find or create a television set to manipulate. Turn it on and experiment with the controls for sound level and intensity, or change the channels. You can even pretend that the TV is voice-controlled, and command it to display certain images. Or, if you want to use a modern update on this technique, you can find or create an Alexa or Echo machine to issue commands to, and enjoy the double bonus that nobody will be tracking your desires in the dream world. Your magic dream television or AI device can even make images real. For example, if you want a sweater to wear, you can command the television to display one or Alexa to order you one, in just your size and the color that matches your eyes. Then you can grab it from the picture and put it on. This device technique is an extremely useful way to practice dream manipulation on a smaller, more manageable scale. Once you master issuing commands to your dream device, you may realize that you don't need the controls or the framing device to realize that you can change your dream.

Scene Spinning

The same spinning technique that stabilizes a dream can be used to completely change the dream scene at hand. Again, simply stick your arms out like a top and start to spin yourself round and round. Focus on the sensation and on the distorted spinning scene. When you stop, you'll find that the dream scene has been transformed. You can even employ this technique with a dream setting in mind before you start to spin: Just yell out the name of a place you'd like to go as a command to your subconscious to transport you there.

Sing or Chant "Om"

There is an incredible listening radar sound dome built by the National Security Agency in Berlin, called Teufelsberg. If you stand in the middle and sing or chant, the unique acoustics of the space send your vocalizations up and around the dome and bounce them back to you, causing a powerful reverberation. It's a heart-stopping experience that I believe has therapeutic powers, and if you have a chance to visit, you definitely should. If not, you can simply chant or sing in a dream, because the dream acoustics are the same as they are in this dome—and your voice will sound better than in real life! Chanting can be a great way to stabilize the dream, especially if you use a mantra, or simply chant "om" to feel the vibrations.

Select a Dream Mantra

A mantra is a sacred sound, word, or phrase that holds psychological or spiritual powers. The word *mantra* comes from Sanskrit: *Man* means "mind," while *tra* means "transport" or "vehicle." It's helpful to choose a mantra that stabilizes a dream, such as "THIS IS MY DREAM" or "I AM IN CONTROL." The power of mantras may come from tapping into our collective unconscious and thousands of years of monks, mystics, nuns, and believers practicing these chants. Similarly, using spells in lucid dreams taken from the famous *Harry Potter* series may also work, given the fact that millions of children across the world truly believe in their power. To help stabilize a dream, you can pick any mantra. But any chant, song, spell, or power word—as long as you believe in it strongly or it has associations with something meaningful to you—can help you manifest a dream figure, trigger an experience, or teleport yourself to another world.

Mirror Reflection

While dreams can be a reflection of your subconscious, mirrors in dreams are not direct reflections of what is placed in front of them. As stated previously, sometimes mirrors can even act as portals in dreams. If you see a mirror in a dream, take a look at the reflection you see. Focusing on what's there will help stabilize the dream. If you're daring, you can try to climb through the mirror. Once, I climbed through a mirror only to tumble down a rabbit hole, like in *Alice in Wonderland*—and then found myself in another dream scene entirely.

HOW TO DEAL WITH LUCIDITY BLOCKAGES

Some people may run into what I call self-created lucidity blockages—people or things in a dream that try to prevent you from having full lucid control. Once, I was flying around a dreamscape in a bout of lucidity, when suddenly I was captured by "dream police" and was then subsequently placed in a floating jail cell with four walls, and no windows or doors. I was frustrated and pounding on the wall, when I realized that this was my dream. I took a few deep breaths, closed my eyes, and then rubbed my hands together to stabilize my dream; then I drew a door with my finger and let myself out. If you find yourself confronted with any dream figure or blockage trying to limit your control, it's likely just a subconscious belief that you couldn't possibly be in full control of a situation surfacing. Simply take a few deep breaths, and remind yourself that this is *your* dream.

LUCID DREAM INCUBATION

Dream incubation essentially consists of planting the seed for an idea to take hold and have it manifest in a dream later on. All you have to do to incubate a dream before going to sleep is to think about what dream setting or situation you'd like to find yourself in later. For example, if you'd like to find yourself in conversation with a person you haven't seen in a long time, you can incubate this dream setting by thinking about that person as you're falling asleep. Or, if you are stuck on a scene in a book you're writing or on a presentation you need to prepare, you can incubate a dream to bring you to where you are stuck. You can kill two birds with one stone by incubating a lucid dream, so that you can not only dream about the subject of your choice, but then control the dream.

Here's how to incubate a lucid dream:

1. **WRITE DOWN THE DREAM YOU'D LIKE TO FIND YOURSELF IN.** Writing is a powerful act, and if you write down in detail the dream scene you want to experience later—such as the place, what you're wearing, who you're with, what objects are around, what you're doing—this will cement in your mind the dream you want to have.

2. **DRAW OR MAKE A COLLAGE OF THE DREAM SCENE YOU DESIRE.** If you're more of a visual person, you can also make a collage of your dream scene, using cutouts from magazines or printed images, or even draw the dream you'd like to find yourself in. I've found that both creating a visual representation of your dream, along with a written description, is doubly effective for dream incubation.

3. **PICK A LUCIDITY TRIGGER.** This is the most important step. In your desired dream scene, add a familiar dream sign to signal to yourself to do a reality check. This way you'll make sure that you will realize that you are dreaming and take control before you continue on in your desired dream scene. It helps to write down or to draw your specific lucidity trigger in this dream.

4. **ONE HOUR BEFORE SLEEPING, FOCUS SOLELY ON THE DREAM SCENE YOU HAVE IN MIND.** If you've written down or created an image of your dream incubation, it may be helpful to place the dream image or write-up underneath your pillow before sleeping.

5. **FALL ASLEEP AND *FEEL* THE EMOTION OF BEING IN THE DREAM.** One powerful technique to ensure that incubation is successful is to fall asleep while imagining and feeling that you are already in the dream that you want to experience. Forget that you're in your bed; focus on the feeling of success that you've incubated a dream, and you'll find yourself in the desired dream.

CONTROLLING YOURSELF VERSUS CONTROLLING THE DREAM

In lucid dreams, there are two types of general control. One is controlling yourself, which is essentially letting your dream take its natural course and simply reacting lucidly and with awareness to events as they unfold. The other is controlling the dream, which focuses on guiding the external events to avoid certain confrontations, without changing your emotions in the dream. For example, if you have a nightmare and are faced with a frightening threat or monster that is chasing you, you can either control yourself by calming your emotions and facing the monster to see what happens, or you can create a trap for the monster to fall into before it can become an urgent threat.

Both methods of control are valid, but I've found from personal experience that first learning to control your own emotions and to face your fears in a dream are far more effective ways of dream control. By just learning to control the dream circumstances, you may be losing out on enlightening insights about yourself, or a chance to confront any past traumas, blockages, or fears you may have. You also then forgo the opportunity to completely master the landscape of your dreams, because you'll be too busy avoiding and navigating a landscape riddled with fears.

After you learn to master yourself while lucid, full dream control will become much easier. And once you've mastered stabilizing your dream and maintaining lucidity, your dream world is literally boundless. Anything that you can imagine is possible in the dream world. In the next chapter, we'll go through some advanced lucid dreaming techniques to guide you through how to best benefit from your newly learned skills.

ADVANCED LUCID DREAMING TECHNIQUES

"Until you make the unconscious conscious,
it will direct your life and you will call it fate."
—C. G. JUNG

A S STATED EARLIER, LUCID DREAMING IS A great avenue for sexual liberation, exploration, and healing. It's an extremely human instinct to want to immediately seek and engage in base pleasures, such as wild sex, especially since lucid dreaming "occurs during a highly activated phase of REM sleep, associated, as a result, with increased vaginal blood flow or penile erections." This physiological priming for desire, paired with the lack of social restraints in the dream world, prompts a lot people to engage in pleasurable lucid dream sex. And lucid dream sex is risk-free and rewarding; you can do it however and with whomever you wish—a celebrity, an Instagram crush, a stranger you saw on the train last week, a random dream character, an ex-coworker . . . the list goes on and on.

While dream hedonism has its advantages, especially if you are blocked in waking life, I've found that the real gratification of lucid dreaming lies beyond this initial instinct to indulge in pleasures of the (dream) flesh. Keep in mind that the immediate gratification of getting what you want in real life can easily dissipate—this is known as the "hedonic treadmill" or "hedonic adaptation," which is the "observed tendency of humans to quickly return to a relatively stable level of happiness despite major positive or negative events or life changes." This theory holds true in the dream world as well. Luckily, given the malleability and endless possibility of the dream world, lucidity allows you to fly off the hedonistic treadmill and into next-level realms of profound experiences and changes.

Below are a few strategies to advance your lucid dreaming skills and delve more deeply into yourself. Some of these simply build on the reasons to lucid dream, as outlined in chapter 3, with more concrete steps and examples of how to reap the benefits of lucidity. As noted earlier, the dream world has no strict rules or limitations. There is no right or wrong way to explore the dreamscape or to achieve your personal goals. These are all mere suggestions and examples of what is possible. Hopefully, these pathways of advanced lucid dreaming will inspire your mind and subconscious to venture on your own journey and to forge new possibilities.

DISCOVER YOUR TRUE SELF

As mentioned earlier, dream mirrors are fascinating objects that shape-shift and can also act as portals in dreams. One way to get to know yourself better is to look and focus on the image in the mirror. Stare at what you see, and notice if you find yourself looking back at your image. If you can see your reflection, you have the opportunity to observe yourself thoroughly. Perhaps your features look distorted, or you can see a part of yourself clearly that you have been neglecting. Once, in a lucid dream I looked in the mirror and saw that my skin was flaking off. It turned out that I had not been drinking enough water. I knew I hadn't been hydrating properly and was drinking too much coffee, but I had ignored this fact, only to have my dream body warn me.

Getting to know yourself takes courage and requires a suspension of self-judgment. One useful exercise I like to do before exploring my true self in a dream is to take an inventory of my current concept of myself. Here's how to do this:

1. **CREATE A LIST OF ALL THE THINGS THAT COMPRISE YOUR IDENTITY.** For example, I would write that I am a writer; that I identify as Asian-American, since both of my parents immigrated to America from Taiwan; that I am a rock climber; that I am a daughter, sister, etc.

2. **WRITE A FEW LINES ABOUT HOW YOU FEEL ABOUT EACH FACET OF YOUR IDENTITY.** Oftentimes, we inherit ideas about who we are from our parents, our society, or others around us. For example, some people may be raised to be

doctors or electricians because they come from generations of professionals in a certain field, or they feel enormous pressure to marry somebody of the same faith or race. It may be a good idea to write out how you feel about each aspect of your identity and to identify the source it comes from.

3. **IN A LUCID DREAM, ASK YOUR REFLECTION WHO YOU ARE.**
You can also ask yourself questions like "What part of myself am I neglecting?" or "What do I need to know about myself?" The answers may surprise you and will give you a lot of good material to meditate on.

4. **TELL YOUR REFLECTION THAT YOU LOVE YOURSELF.**
This may sound cheesy, but a lot of our judgments and insecurities simply come from a lack of self-love. One psychologist I admire, Marisa Peer, is famous for her "I am enough" movement. She espouses the idea that we believe the words we speak, so if we tell ourselves that we love ourselves, it has a profound effect on our self-image. I've found that this method is even more powerful during a lucid dream state.

CONQUER NIGHTMARES AND ANXIETY DREAMS

One of the old, recurring anxiety dreams that used to plague me frequently was the rather unpleasant experience of losing my teeth. In these dreams, I felt horrified to feel my teeth crumble in my mouth. Some dream dictionaries contend that this common dream is symbolic of a fear of change. The next time I found myself inside a dream where my molars were disintegrating inside my mouth, instead of succumbing to the fear, I became lucid and then took a good look at myself in the mirror. I spat out the morsels of my teeth, rinsed out my mouth and then looked in the dream mirror—only to see that I had grown a newer set of white, strong teeth! I had confronted my fear of change and then saw a symbolic representation that change, while scary, can be for the better and leave room for growth.

Here are a few strategies to deal with nightmares or recurring anxiety dreams:

1. **REVISE THE NIGHTMARE AS SOON AS YOU WAKE UP.** As soon as you wake up from an unpleasant dream, go over in your mind what you would have liked to happen instead in your dream. It can be helpful to write down revisions, and simply by doing that with a calm state of mind, you can analyze the dream better without the charged emotions from within the dream.

2. **RECOGNIZE YOUR EMOTIONS OF FEAR AND THEN BREATHE THROUGH THEM.** If something or someone is chasing you, or if something terrible is happening to you in your dream, simply try pausing and not reacting. Oftentimes, controlling your emotions and accepting the situation without panicking or giving in to fear can clarify the point

of the nightmare, so that you can see through your fear and directly to the problem at hand.

3. **CONFRONT YOUR DREAM ENEMY OR MONSTER.** Many dreamers report that if, mid-chase, they stop and confront their pursuer, the monster that was so menacing is diminished to a monster that's actually afraid, too. You can also ask your monster directly what it is that he wants, or ask the dream its meaning. Once, in a recurring dream I had in which I couldn't run any faster, no matter how hard I tried, I asked out loud, "What is stopping me from running?" Suddenly I saw my boyfriend at the time, holding onto my ankles. I realized that our relationship was toxic, and eventually ended it between us, which also ended the frustrating dreams.

IMPROVE YOUR CREATIVITY OR SOLVE A PROBLEM

As a writer, I've had some lucid dreams in which I meet the characters in fiction pieces that I'm working on. Before I go to bed, I incubate a dream in which I want to meet and talk with a certain fictional character, and then, during the dream, I'll ask her questions about what she wants and what drives her, or anything else that I may be stuck on in a certain draft. No matter what your medium of expression is, there are a few strategies you can employ in lucid dreaming to increase creativity or to solve a problem.

Here are a few ways to improve your creative problem-solving:

Problem-Solving: Ask a Mentor for Help

One famous account told by Stephen LaBerge and Howard Rheingold demonstrates how a computer programmer would work with Albert Einstein in his lucid dreams. After having collaborated with one of the world's most famous geniuses, the programmer would wake up and immediately record the dream work done—to an astonishing 99 percent accuracy. Sometimes, you can just have a lucid dream chat with a person you admire for reassurance, like memory champion Yänjaa Wintersoul. She told me about having several dreams in which she has tea with Oprah and leaves with the reassurance that good things are coming. Lucid dream mentors can also be good for decision making. Yänjaa told me over email, "When I was going through a particularly difficult decision, a version of God who was George Clooney called me to his office and when I asked if George Clooney was God he said, 'No, this is just the shape you feel most comfortable with accepting as a concept of God right now.' I made the right decision after that meeting."

Creating Art from Dreams

In a lucid landscape, you can paint with your finger and saliva. You can conduct an orchestra, or envision a magical jukebox that will play music from the depths of your own imagination. Paul McCartney famously woke up with the tune of "Yesterday" playing in his head, left over from a dream. You can also literally take your dreams and turn them into art—I once had a session with an artist friend of mine, Anna Broujean, in which we created a short story composed of a mash-up of lines from dreams that we had each recorded.

Meditating in a Lucid Dream

If you've already established a regular meditation practice in waking life, then prepare yourself for an intense experience. While meditating in real life can take a few minutes for some of us (longer for others, shorter for the more experienced) to reach a flow state where we are simply connected to our breath, meditating during a dream seems to fast-track us to a bliss-like experience. In several lucid dreams where I've sat down to meditate, I immediately felt a vibration, paired with beautiful geometric hypnagogic imagery. I was immersed in a joyful sensation, as if I were vibrating on a higher level with the entire universe.

Here's how to meditate in a lucid dream:

1. **ESTABLISH A MEDITATION PRACTICE.** As noted before, a daily meditation practice doesn't require anything except your own body and five minutes a day. Creating a habit of meditating will help your dream meditation.

2. **INCUBATE A LUCID DREAM WITH INTENTION TO MEDITATE.** One of my strategies for incubating meditative dreams is to write the phrase "Lucid Meditation Tonight" on a piece of paper before going to bed.

3. **AS SOON AS YOU REACH LUCIDITY, CLOSE YOUR EYES.**

   Unlike in the real world, meditating in a dream can be as easy as closing your eyes, no matter where you are or how your body is positioned. As soon as I close my eyes in a lucid dream and focus on my breathing, I feel that I'm quickly transported into a higher state of consciousness.

❈ ❈ ❈

Another benefit of meditating inside a lucid dream is that it can have a tremendous positive effect on your waking meditation practice, too.

Practicing Tibetan Dream Yoga

Tibetan dream yoga is essentially lucid dreaming, because it's defined as a wakeful awareness while you are dreaming. But dream yoga is far more spiritual than hedonistic, and it involves active reflection and meditation on yourself and your life. Like yoga, dream yoga is a practice that is meant to help you evolve physically, mentally, and spiritually. But the ultimate goal of Tibetan dream yoga is to help those who practice it enter and pass through the bardo, which is the state between death and rebirth. Dzogchen teacher Namkhai Norbu explains in his book *Dream Yoga and the Practice of Natural Light* that the after-death state known as the "chonyid bardo" entails vivid, dreamlike hallucinations. For lucid dreamers, it is in the bardo that we are given the opportunity to recognize the true, illusory nature of these hallucinations and thereby transcend death by perhaps escaping the cycle of samsara.

Here are a few ways to deepen your Tibetan dream yoga practice:

1. **RECOGNIZE AND TRANSFORM THE ORDINARY HABITS OF THE MIND.** Which dreams do you keep finding yourself in, and in what kind of situations? How can you resolve each recurring dream or issue so you can move forward in your dreams? Tip: It's equally useful to do a similar analysis of what kind of recurring situations you find yourself in during your waking life.

2. **RECOGNIZE AND REMOVE LIMITATIONS IN YOUR DREAMS.** The mind is innately creative and compassionate, and it's useful to put this into practice during a dream. For example, you can practice multiplying things in a dream, such as flowers or butterflies or kittens. Take one and then make ten and then thousands, until there is an endless amount of beauty extending toward every corner of space.

3. **IMAGINE YOUR BED AS A HEALING TEMPLE.** Another Tibetan technique is to imagine your bed as a large, luminous lotus bud or a small temple that has healing and regenerating light properties. As you sleep, imagine bathing in the healing light of that space, and feeling that you are infused with all the positive energy of the universe.

HOW TO ENTER THE "DREAM VOID"

Some studies show that it may even be possible to be conscious during non-REM sleep. One study, which involved an Indian master of yoga meditation, Swāmī Rāma of the Himālayas, showed an "ability to enter the deepest, non-REM delta wave sleep while maintaining awareness both internally and of one's surroundings (yoga-nidra)." Dr. Clare Johnson also writes about the dream void in her book, *Llewellyn's Complete Book of Lucid Dreaming*: "I believe that we probably all experience the void every night, and likely at different stages of the sleep cycle . . . I see it as a natural gap between dreams . . . If we do become lucid, the void can be a fascinating and perplexing experience." For anyone who has tried and benefited from sensory deprivation tanks (tanks filled with salt water at body temperature that participants enter naked, to simulate being in outer space with no sense of touch, sight, smell, or anything else), the void is a free version of floating that's available to you anytime you sleep. The void is a relaxing space where we are freed from our bodies and subconscious projections that is the dream and waking world; it is a place where we can experiment with any sort of magic, such as constructing images or sound from nothing, or completely relax and be at one with a larger underlying reality.

Here are several techniques to enter the dream void:

1. **DO A BACKFLIP.** Dr. Clare Johnson writes that one of her favorite ways to enter the void is to do a backflip as soon as

she achieves lucidity, with the intention of going there. To do a backflip, simply jump up with your arms up straight, then bring your knees to your chest while leaning back.

2. **MEDITATE WITH INTENTION.** Before meditating in a dream, you can say out loud to yourself, "Now, I'm entering the void." Close your eyes and expect to find the void when you do so.

3. **FIND A PORTAL.** This can be a mirror, a door, a closet, a manhole, a tunnel—anything can be a portal to the void, as long as you open it with the intention of finding the void.

BATHE IN THE "LUCID LIGHT"

Another dimension we can explore in the dream world is the "lucid light." A term coined by Dr. Clare Johnson, *lucid light* is "pure conscious awareness, and as such it seems to be the energy of the universe and beyond, the underlying oneness that binds everyone and everything together." This light, she speculates, may be the same light some people describe in hypnagogia, lucid dreams, out-of-body experiences, and near-death experiences: "Lucid Light is our baseline state of consciousness: this is the state from which all forms and matter emerge . . . this is the light we emerge from as conscious beings, and it is the light we return to at the moment of dying."

Along with many anecdotes of seeing a "white light" during near-death experiences, doctors in Canada confirmed that after the death of one patient, the individual "appeared to experience the same kind of brain waves (delta wave bursts) we get during deep sleep" for as long as ten minutes after the absence of a pulse. But the concept of white light as a mystic source has been around for a long time. In Tibetan Buddhism, "clear light" is the "subtlest level of mind," and has qualities of "Buddha-nature." In the Bible, one of the most famous and well-known citations from Genesis 1:3 is "And God said, Let there be light: and there was light." Physicist Russell Targ argues that "quantum hologram [the idea that our reality is illusory and projected from a 3D surface] is an order of pure beingness, pure frequency—perhaps the essential Light itself—which transcends all specifications and knows neither 'here' nor 'there.' It is the realm from which the forms of reality are engendered, pervading everything, and potentially totally available at any particular part of our reality."

Thus, if every interaction contains this light, it may be possible to experience the "lucid light" in various states of consciousness, by meditating or even simply by relaxing. Finding and bathing in the lucid light may help increase your awareness of pure consciousness, and perhaps even become a transformative and profound spiritual experience. It's a worthy venture to experience lucid light in a lucid dream, and, for obvious reasons, it is an easier pathway than having a near-death experience.

Here are several techniques to experience the lucid light:

1. **INCUBATE A LUCID LIGHT DREAM EXPERIENCE.** Before going to bed, write down your intention to have a lucid dream

bathed in the lucid light. Focus and concentrate on this intention as you fall asleep.

2. **LOOK FOR WHITE LIGHT IN A DREAM.** Sometimes, balls of white light will appear in dreams, perhaps to signal to your consciousness to become more aware. Pay attention to these signs, and if you're already lucid, you can imagine a ball of white light between your dream hands.

3. **ENTER FROM THE VOID.** After entering the void space, I've personally found that, from there, it's very easy to enter the lucid light by just closing your eyes and opening them to expect the light. The concept of the void and the lucid light remind me of yin and yang; they are at once inseparable and contradictory, two halves of the same coin.

4. **MEDITATE.** One easy way to directly access the lucid light is to close your eyes and meditate in a lucid dream, focusing on the energy and light within your dream body.

GOING BEYOND ADVANCED LUCID DREAMING

Lucid dreaming can profoundly transform our lives by allowing us to discover who we are and to feel empowered to become the person we want to be and to live the life that we'd like. By conquering our nightmares and quelling our anxieties, the mind will become far freer to focus on the present moment and the road ahead leading to our individual goals. And by tapping into our innate creativity and imagination, we can problem-solve and forge paths to our goals that may have been previously unseen or blocked by old or limiting ideas. We can meditate and experience the bliss of feeling nothing at all in the void between dreams, and, in the same way, tap into the idea of pure consciousness as lucid light. But the possibilities of lucid dreaming do not end there. By exploring the world of lucid dreaming even more deeply, the line between dreams and reality begins to blur. Some lucid dreamers have reportedly healed their own physical bodies or those of others. In addition, some have experienced dream telepathy, out-of-body experiences, and other paranormal events in which reality becomes nothing but another malleable dream, controlled by our own consciousness.

LUCID DREAMING, TELEPATHY, HEALING, AND OTHER POSSIBILITIES

"*Either one does not dream, or one does so interestingly.
One should learn to spend one's waking life in the same way:
not at all, or interestingly.*"

—Friedrich Nietzsche

T HE DEEPER ONE DIVES INTO THE DREAM world, the stranger and more interesting reality becomes. Once I began lucid dreaming, I came across stranger and stranger experiences. In one lucid dream, I was flying and talking to a dream character I had happened upon mid-flight. She and I began talking, and she identified herself as a lucid dreamer. While we introduced ourselves, she told me that she lived in Bushwick, a neighborhood in Brooklyn—not too far from where I once lived (at the time of the dream, I had moved to Denver). I was stunned, and then asked her to give me her address and to describe the building. Later, when I woke up, I googled the address and looked at the street view, and was astounded to see that the building I saw on my screen matched her description of it exactly.

PRECOGNITIVE DREAMS, REMOTE VIEWING, AND TELEPATHY

Other strange dreams involved synchronicities or precognitive events. When I was six years old, right before a school year began in which, for the first time, I was old enough to stay the entire day and thus throughout lunchtime, I had a dream where I was in line to be served lunch. I remember the faces of the two lunch ladies, as they were called, serving me a bagel with cream cheese. The next day, when I went to school, I remember feeling shocked because the faces of the women serving me lunch—whom I had never seen before—were the same exact faces I had seen in my dream! In another synchronous dream I had, I had broken my braces off my teeth. I didn't think much of the dream, since I didn't have braces at that point in my life, just a small, permanent retainer on the interior backside of my bottom set of teeth. However, the next day, I was on a subway platform waiting for the train when I bit into an apple and then broke my retainer.

Another strange dream coincidence involved my mother. At the time of the dream, my mother was back in her homeland of Taiwan, while I was living in New York. One night, I had a dream in which she appeared to me, in a panic, asking me the number for 911. I replied to her in my dream, "obviously, it's 9-1-1, Mom!" and then woke up. Shortly after, I gave her a call, only to discover that my grandma had fallen earlier that day (Taiwan is twelve hours ahead of New York time), and my mother had kept incorrectly dialing 911, because in Taiwan, the emergency number is 119!

I am not alone in experiencing these strange incidences where dreams blend into real life and vice versa. There's been a lot of research done on the intersections of dreams, out-of-body experiences, remote viewing, telepathy, and other "psychic abilities," which defy the bounds of what is normally accepted as possible.

Precognitive dreams are dreams that accurately predict the future. Throughout history, there have been reports of people dreaming about events that later happened in real life. One striking incident involves the catastrophic collapse of a colliery spoil tip (a pile of waste material removed after mining), known as the Aberfan disaster, in which over a hundred lives were lost. Many of the dead were children, and there were also reports of precognitive dreams before the event. One reported dream was written by Glannant Jones, a local minister, which was signed by a young girl's parents:

> The day before the disaster she said to her mother, "Mummy, let me tell you about my dream last night." Her mother answered gently, "Darling, I've no time. Tell me again later." The child replied, "No Mummy, you must listen. I dreamt I went to school and there was no school there. Something black had come down all over it!"

While a few examples don't imply that dreams can predict the future, it is an interesting thought experiment to assume that, in some cases, dreams can predict the future. If this is the case, I wonder, could we control our dreams as a way to control the future?

Test Your Own Precognitive Dreams

By keeping a dream log, you'll be able to flip back and look through your dreams to see if any of them were precognitive. I've found that by simply engaging with lucid dreaming more often, precognitive dreams happened at a higher frequency. However, I've also flipped back through to dreams that I had more than a year ago, only to find that I had dreamed about things or conversations that happened later in real life!

To identify a precognitive dream, analyze it carefully to make sure it wasn't caused by any activity or influence from the previous day or any desires or anxieties. Most precognitive dreams have a distinct clarity and contain bizarre or unfamiliar material.

Dream Telepathy

Not only can some dreams foretell the future, but it seems that it is possible to communicate with other people through dreams, too. In the 1960s, the sleep laboratory of New York's Maimonides Medical Center carried out ESP (extrasensory perception) experiments that studied precognition. Dreamers were to describe dreams of a target—the image of an object—before it was selected, with stunning results: "Five out of eight experiments were direct hits, and two more were close matches—with odds against of 5000–1." They also studied telepathy, where a "sender" attempted to send images to a "receiver" who slept in another room, and his sleep was recorded with standard EEG leads. Once the sleeper was in the REM stage, he was awakened and reported his dream, which was then assessed by independent judges to determine if the dream contained any of the images sent by the sender.

Dr. Clare Johnson, a lifelong avid lucid dreamer, had her own preconceived notions of what is possible blown away at a 2004 IASD (International Association for the Study of Dreams) dream telepathy contest. Similar to the Maimonides experiments, a telepathic sender publicly chose one of four sealed envelopes, each of which contained a different picture that nobody had seen before. Then, the sender opened the envelope in privacy and subsequently spent the night trying to transmit the image. Participants then looked for the images in their dreams and recorded the results, which were compared later. Dr. Johnson entered the contest, skeptical of dream telepathy, only to then have a bizarrely intricate dream of a woman shouting the word tree. After she woke up, she still wasn't convinced that the tree image was the correct answer, but then it turned out that not only had she won first place in the contest, but it was the "most direct hit they'd ever had."

What Dr. Johnson accomplished is comparable to the stunning feats done by remote viewing, which is the ability to see or sense information about a target without access to the senses. Physicist Russell Targ coined the term *remote viewing* and has written extensively about the topic in his wonderful book *Limitless Mind: A Guide to Remote Viewing and Transformation of Consciousness*. The remote-viewing research, performed at SRI International (formerly known as Stanford Research Institute) and Princeton University, "showed conclusively that remote viewing exists, with a departure from chance expectation of 1010 (odds of one in ten billion)."

It seems that remote viewing—the ability to describe and experience events and locations that are blocked from ordinary perception—may simply be another form of consciousness, similar to the dream state, in which we can access and transmit information in ways we did not think possible. It's exciting to think about what other extraordinary things our minds are capable of when limitations are lifted.

> *"The choice of where we put our attention is ultimately our most powerful freedom. Our choice of attitude and focus affects not only our own perceptions and experiences, but also the experiences and behaviors of others."*
>
> —RUSSELL TARG

Try Dream Mind Reading with a Friend

By playing telepathy games, you can exercise your intuition and boost your ability to stay present with an open mind during your dreams. Here's a game you can play with a partner.

1. **CUT OUT FOUR CARDS AND HAVE ONE PERSON DRAW FOUR DIFFERENT IMAGES ON THEM.** Make sure that they're fairly simple shapes, like stars, triangles, circles, or wavy lines.

2. **PICK ONE CARD AND SEND THE IMAGE THROUGHOUT THE NIGHT.** Let your friend know which shapes are on the cards, but not which one you've picked to send. Throughout the night, focus on dreaming about the shape you've picked and imagine sending it to your friend. Your partner will try to incubate a dream in which she receives the image.

3. **GET THE RESULTS IN THE MORNING AND SWITCH PLACES.** In the morning, phone your friend to see what image she received in her dream. You can also play this game again by switching places, and you can swap out the images on the cards, too.

❖ Conclusion ❖
WAKING UP TO REALITY AND LUCID LIVING

"Everything you can imagine is real."
—Pablo Picasso

ONE OF THE PASSAGES THAT HAS STUCK WITH me the most in all the literature I've read on lucid dreaming is from Stephen LaBerge and Howard Rheingold's book *Exploring the World of Lucid Dreaming,* in which he recounts a workshop on Tibetan Buddhism he participated in at the Esalen Institute in the 1970s. It was led by Tibetan teacher Tarthang Tulku, also known as Rinpoche, who apparently did not speak English fluently at the time.

> Rinpoche would indicate the world around us with a casual sweep of the hand and portentously announce: "This . . . dream!" Then he would laugh some more and pointing at me

or some other person or object, rather mysteriously it seemed, he would insist: "This dream!" followed by more laughter. Rinpoche managed to get the idea across to us that we were to attempt to think of all of our experiences as dreams and to try to maintain unbroken continuity of consciousness between the two states of sleeping and waking.

What if Rinpoche quite literally meant that waking reality was a dream? What if we were indeed to realize that there is no difference between the real world and the dream world? What if complete awareness and focus on the present moment could change our waking life? What if we could control our waking reality the same way that we control our dreams?

THE POWER OF AWARENESS AND LUCID LIVING

Once we learn the art of lucid dreaming, I think it's only natural that we should pursue what I call lucid living. It's the reflection and extension of lucid dreaming, so we're just as aware and in awe of what we see in front of us while we're awake. It's to appreciate every moment, and to be extremely present and engaged, without worrying about the future or rehashing the past. It's about waking up to the fact that we are free to do whatever we want in this life, to dream big dreams without limitations, and that we are in complete control of our emotions and our reactions.

Here are my principles for lucid living:

1. **TREAT OTHERS AS A REFLECTION OF YOURSELF, AND TREAT THEM AS YOU WOULD TREAT YOURSELF.** This includes individuals, animals, and especially the earth. Recognize that anyone or anything that triggers hate or disgust in you is likely a reflection of your own being, and that you simply need to work on that aspect of yourself. If other people are reflections of yourself and if we are all connected, then it's important to talk about the possibility of dreams and the power of lucid dreaming with everyone you love, and even with strangers. The more that we can help other people wake up, the more than we can wake up ourselves.

2. **FOCUS AND TRAIN YOUR THOUGHTS, BECAUSE OUR THOUGHTS MAKE UP OUR REALITY.** Focus and meditation are very important and key not only to maintaining a calm and peaceful life, but also to reaching any goals that we want to accomplish.

3. **KNOW YOURSELF AND YOUR GOALS CLEARLY—WITH NO LIMITATIONS.** Lucidity means awareness, and to live lucidly we must be able to strip down desires that have been implanted by society or others, and to live true to our own self. Living lucidly means that we are living in tune with our own desires, and we don't pay attention to any external or self-imposed limitations on what is possible.

4. **BEAUTY CAN BE FOUND EVERYWHERE AND IN EVERY ACTION.** In the dream world, nothing is mundane because it's thrilling just to exist in it and to be aware of what is possible. Similarly, in the waking world, everything can be done with an intent to create beauty or peace. Even washing dishes or setting the table can become therapeutic, a matter of art or joy, when viewed through this lens.

5. **LIFE IS BUT A DREAM THAT WE ARE IN CONTROL OF.** As the mystic Neville Goddard wrote, "You are free to choose the concept you will accept of yourself. Therefore, you possess the power of intervention, the power which enables you to alter the course of your future. The process of rising from your present concept to a higher concept of yourself is the means of all true progress. The higher concept is waiting for you to incarnate it in the world of experience."

Dreaming is such an integral part of what makes us human, and indeed our dreams have deeply shaped our history and the world as we see it today. Personally, I think that the discovery of lucid dreaming is one of the biggest advances we've ever made—it's like discovering the power of imagination, and how things are created. Imagine if all of us paid more attention to our dreams, and invoked our latent power to lucid dream. It would create an incredible ripple effect of wellness, because, first of all, people would become healthier, by eating more balanced diets and establishing healthier sleeping routines. Then, by increasing awareness and focus, and training ourselves to lucid dream, the capacity to heal and transform ourselves is endless. People would be able to express themselves sexually; problem-solve creatively; heal past traumas or even their physical body; experience freedom of movement; experience what it's like to live in another person's skin; have a transformative, near-psychedelic experience; and even find their own voices or sing therapeutically. By exploring their creativity and liberty in dreams, people would open up their horizons of what is possible. Limitations and self-restrictions would fall away.

With people today exploring avenues like out-of-body experiences, remote viewing, and psychic lucid dream communication, it seems that dreams are the frontiers of what is possible in this world. This is exciting because it means that, without limitations, we would be armed with new tools to solve the problems that plague our earth and our society; among them, racism, poverty, loneliness, suicide, sickness, greed, and fear. But perhaps the solutions for our global problems lie within each individual. If we ever realized the true nature of reality as a dream, there would be no reason for us to get upset or to hurt others. Because in training ourselves to lucid dream, we'd realize that the dream world was a reflection of ourselves. There would be nothing to fear, as long as we were in control of our own emotions, focus, and imagination.

My hope is that anyone who reads this book can let go of their judgments and attachments to restrictions. I've been in heated discussions before with extremely intelligent people, arguing over the nature of reality. Some people like to focus on harsh "realities," limitations, and the negative aspects of life. I certainly don't dismiss or ignore those. Nightmares do exist on this planet, but, like the ones that haunt us in our sleep, I do not believe that they are invincible. They can be conquered. We can overcome them and any difficulty as we do in lucid dreams, by confronting them with love and by changing our own inner state. My wish is for everyone to take a moment to focus on the possibilities of lucid dreaming, and to realize that there is a very good chance that life is nothing but a dream. If that is the case, what would we have to lose by focusing on the magic of our imagination and dreams? What beautiful dreams could we turn into our waking reality?

Imagine waking up, day after day, dream after dream, to realize that everything you see before you is a reflection of your inner thoughts and feelings. And the one power each of us always has, which nobody can take away from us, is the power to control how we think and how we feel. Being aware of this is the truest lucidity there is.

NOTES

CHAPTER 1: WHAT IS A LUCID DREAM?

PAGE 3. "But one scientific study conducted in 2015 . . .": B. Herlin, S. Leu-Semenescu, C. Chaumereuil, and I. Arnulf, "Evidence That Non-Dreamers Do Dream: A REM Sleep Behaviour Disorder Model," *Journal of Sleep Research* 24 (2015): 602–609. doi:10.1111/jsr.12323.

PAGE 3. "A German study from 2011 . . .": M. Schredl and D. Erlacher, "Frequency of Lucid Dreaming in a Representative German Sample," Sleep Laboratory, Central Institute of Mental Health, Mannheim, Germany (2011). doi: 10.2466/09.PMS.112.1.104–108.

PAGE 4. "A person can have anywhere from . . .": National Sleep Foundation, "How Often Do We Dream?" (2020). Accessed April 15, 2020. https://www.sleep.org/articles/how-often-dreams/.

PAGE 4. "One researcher at the Federal University . . .": U. Voss, R. Holzmann, I. Tuin, and A. Hobson, "Lucid Dreaming: A State of Consciousness with Features of Both Waking and Non-Lucid Dreaming," *SLEEP* 32, no. 9 (2009): 1191–1200. doi: 10.1093/sleep/32.9.1191.

PAGE 4. "Another study, conducted in 2009 . . .": S. A. Mota-Rolim, and J. F. Araujo, "Neurobiology and Clinical Implications of Lucid Dreaming," *Medical Hypotheses* (2013). http://dx.doi.org/10.1016/j.mehy.2013.04.049.

PAGE 4: "Exactly how gamma waves are generated . . .": "What are Brain Waves?" ©Symphonic Mind Ltd. Accessed April 15, 2020. https://brainworksneurotherapy.com/what-are-brainwaves.

CHAPTER 2: A BRIEF HISTORY OF LUCID DREAMING

PAGE 9. "A letter he penned . . .": Saint Augustine, "Letter 159 (A.D. 415)." *Church Fathers New Advent.* Accessed April 24, 2020. https://www.newadvent.org/fathers/1102159.htm.

PAGE 9. "Eminent Tibetan lama Tenzin Wangyal Rinpoche ...": "Milam Sleep Yoga: Lucid Dreaming Can Bring Us Closer to Experiencing Non-Dualistic 'Reality' Than Waking Meditation," *Buddha Weekly* (January 24, 2019). https://buddhaweekly.com/milam-sleep-yoga-lucid-dreaming-can-bring-us-closer-experiencing-non-dualistic-reality-waking-meditation/.

PAGE 11. "He describes his own lucid dreams ...": https://doi.apa.org/getdoi.cfm?doi=10.1037/h0062105.

PAGE 16. "Dream researcher Ursula Voss and her team ...": Virginia Hughes, "Seeking Roots of Consciousness, Scientists Make Dreamers Self-Aware," *National Geographic* (May 17, 2016). Accessed April 24, 2020. https://www.nationalgeographic.com/news/2014/5/140511-lucid-dreaming-sleep-nightmares-consciousness-brain/.

PAGE 16. "In 2013, neuroscientist Yukiyasu Kamitani recorded ...": Nina Strochlic, "Scientists Are Trying to See Our Dreams," *National Geographic* (April 27, 2017). Accessed April 24, 2020. https://www.nationalgeographic.com/magazine/2017/05/explore-dream-mapping/.

PAGE 16 "MIT Dream Lab ..." "Project Overview Dormio: Interfacing with Dreams." MIT Media Lab. Accessed May 26, 2020. https://www.media.mit.edu/projects/sleep-creativity/overview/.

CHAPTER 3: WHY LUCID DREAM?

PAGE 25. "One study of Swedish choir singers ...": Anna Haensch, "When Choirs Sing, Many Hearts Beat As One," *NPR* (July 10, 2013). Accessed April 24, 2020. https://www.npr.org/sections/health-shots/2013/07/09/200390454/when-choirs-sing-many-hearts-beat-as-one.

PAGE 26. "One 2011 study on dream movement ...": Dresler M, Koch SP, Wehrle R, et al. Dreamed movement elicits activation in the sensorimotor cortex. *Curr Biol.* 2011; 21(21):1833-1837. Accessed April 24, 2020. doi: 10.1016/j.cub.2011.09.029.

PAGE 26. "Further, a 2000 study conducted by Stephen LaBerge ...": Stephen LaBerge and P. G. Zimbardo. "Smooth Tracking Eye-Movements Discriminate Both Dreaming and Perception from Imagination," Toward a Science of Consciousness Conference IV (April 10, 2000). http://www.lucidity.com/Tucson2000abs.html.

PAGE 27. "One 2012 study of lucid dreamers . . .": M. Schädlich and D. Erlacher, "Applications of Lucid Dreams: An Online Study," *International Journal of Dream Research* 5, no. 2(2012): 134–138. https://doi.org/10.11588/ijodr.2012.2.9505.

PAGE 27. "A study at the University of Lincoln . . .": Matthew Jenkin, "Stumped for Ideas? Lucid Dreaming Lets You Work While You Sleep." *Guardian* (September 20, 2016). https://www.theguardian.com/small-business-network/2016/sep/20/stumped-ideas-lucid-dreaming-work-while-sleep.

PAGE 29. "The idea of reenacting past trauma . . .": G. C. Harb, J. A. Brownlow, and R. J. Ross, "Posttraumatic Nightmares and Imagery Rehearsal: The Possible Role of Lucid Dreaming," *Dreaming* 26, no. 3 (2016): 238–249. https://doi.org/10.1037/drm0000030.

PAGE 29. "While the Greeks used sleeping temples . . .": "Hypnosis in Ancient Civilizations," The Cuyamungue Institute. Accessed April 16, 2020. https://www.cuyamungueinstitute.com/articles-and-news/hypnosis-in-ancient-civilizations/.

PAGE 29-30. "Later, at the 2007 PsiberDreaming Conference . . .": "Mind-Body Healing through Dreamwork," IASD Documents (2007). https://asdreams.org/psi2007/papers/edkellogg.htm.

PAGE 30. "There have been other reports of successful uses of lucid . . .": "Lucid Dream Healing Experiences: Firsthand Accounts," IASD Documents. Association for the Study of Dreams (1998). https://asdreams.org/documents/1999_kellogg_lucid-healing.htm.

CHAPTER 4: LAYING THE FOUNDATIONS FOR A LUCID DREAM

PAGE 38. "Some people with sensitivity to EMFs . . .": Malka N. Halgamuge, "Pineal Melatonin Level Disruption in Humans Due to Electromagnetic Fields and ICNIRP Limits," *Radiation Protection Dosimetry* (May 2013). doi: 10.1093/rpd/ncs255.

PAGE 39. "The average American spends more . . .": Rani Molla, "Americans Spent about 3.5 Hours per Day on Their Phones Last Year—a Number That Keeps Going Up Despite the 'Time Well Spent' Movement," *Vox* (January 6, 2020). https://www.vox.com/recode/2020/1/6/21048116/tech-companies-time-well-spent-mobile-phone-usage-data.

PAGE 43. "One study showed that certain amounts . . .": I. Karacan, J. I. Thornby, M. Anch, G. H. Booth, R. L. Williams, and P. J. Salis, "Dose-Related Sleep Disturbances

Induced by Coffee and Caffeine," *Clinical Pharmacology and Therapeutics*, U.S. National Library of Medicine (December 1976). doi: 10.1002/cpt1976206682.

PAGE 44. "But a recent 2018 study showed . . .": "Vitamin B6 Helps People Recall Their Dreams," ScienceDaily (April 27, 2018). https://www.sciencedaily.com/releases/2018/04/180427100258.htm.

PAGE 44. "Another study from 2013 found that a varied diet . . .": "Eat to Dream: Study Shows Dietary Nutrients Associated with Certain Sleep Patterns," ScienceDaily (February 6, 2013). https://www.sciencedaily.com/releases/2013/02/130206093542.htm.

PAGE 44. "Nearly one in two Americans are . . .": "Nearly One in Two Americans Takes Prescription Drugs: Survey." Bloomberg.com (May 8, 2019). https://www.bloomberg.com/news/articles/2019-05-08/nearly-one-in-two-americans-takes-prescription-drugs-survey.

PAGE 44. "People who are attempting to quit smoking . . .": F. Page, G. Coleman, and R. Conduit, "The Effect of Transdermal Nicotine Patches on Sleep and Dreams," *Physiology & Behavior* (July 30, 2006). doi: 10.1016/j.physbeh.2006.04.009.

PAGE 44. "Some treatments for Alzheimer's disease . . .": Peter Dockrill, "A New Method for Having Lucid Dreams Has Been Discovered by Scientists," ScienceAlert (August 21, 2018). https://www.sciencealert.com/scientists-figured-out-new-technique-having-lucid-dreams-acetylcholine-galantamine-alzheimer-s-drug.

PAGE 44. "Interestingly, the sleeping aid pill Ambien . . .": Kareem Yasin, "The Bizarre Side Effects of Taking Ambien," Healthline Media (August 30, 2018). https://www.healthline.com/health/side-effects-of-taking-ambien#3.

CHAPTER 5: WAYS TO LUCIDITY

PAGE 57. "But unlike in dreams, one 2013 study . . .": Jana Speth, Clemens Frenzel, and Ursula Voss, "A Differentiating Empirical Linguistic Analysis of Dreamer Activity in Reports of EEG-Controlled REM-Dreams and Hypnagogic Hallucinations," *Consciousness and Cognition* (August 7, 2013). doi: https://doi.org/10.1016/j.concog.2013.07.003.

CHAPTER 6: LIVING THE LUCID DREAM

PAGE 69. "'the system of the brain that integrates . . .'": LaBerge and Rheingold, *Exploring the World of Lucid Dreaming*, p. 143.

PAGE 70. "German researcher Paul Tholey discovered . . .": Paul Tholey, "Consciousness and Abilities of Dream Characters Observed during Lucid Dreaming," *Perceptual and Motor Skills* (April 1989). doi: 10.2466/pms.1989.68.2.567.

PAGE 75. "The word *mantra* comes from Sanskrit . . .": Tris Thorp, "What Is a Mantra?" Chopra Center (March 10, 2018). https://chopra.com/articles/what-is-a-mantra.

CHAPTER 7: ADVANCED LUCID DREAMING TECHNIQUES

PAGE 81. "lucid dreaming 'occurs during a highly activated' . . .": LaBerge and Rheingold, *Exploring the World of Lucid Dreaming*, p. 171.

PAGE 82. "Keep in mind that the immediate gratification of . . .": Stephanie Rosenbloom, "But Will It Make You Happy?" *New York Times* (August 7, 2010). https://www.nytimes.com/2010/08/08/business/08consume.html?pagewanted=all.

PAGE 91. "One study, which involved an Indian master . . .": Stephen Parker, "Training Attention for Conscious Non-REM Sleep: The Yogic Practice of Yoga-Nidrā and Its Implications for Neuroscience Research," *Progress in Brain Research* (January 3, 2019). doi: 10.1016/bs.pbr.2018.10.016.

PAGE 91. "Dr. Clare Johnson also writes about the dream void . . .": Clare R. Johnson, *Llewellyn's Complete Book of Lucid Dreaming: A Comprehensive Guide to Promote Creativity, Overcome Sleep Disturbances & Enhance Health and Wellness* (Woodbury MN: Llewellyn Worldwide Ltd., 2017), p. 327.

PAGE 92. "doctors in Canada confirmed . . .": Bec Crew, "Brain Activity Has Been Recorded as Much as 10 Minutes after Death," ScienceAlert (October 5, 2018). https://www.sciencealert.com/brain-activity-recorded-as-much-as-10-minutes-after-death-human-science.

PAGE 93. "In Tibetan Buddhism, 'clear light' . . .": Alexander Berzin, "Buddha-Nature and the Clear Light Mind," Berzin Archives. Accessed April 16, 2020.

https://studybuddhism.com/en/advanced-studies/lam-rim/buddha-nature/
buddha-nature-and-the-clear-light-mind.

PAGE 93. "Physicist Russell Targ argues that . . .": Russell Targ, *Limitless Mind:
A Guide to Remote Viewing and Transformation of Consciousness* (Novato, CA: New
World Library, 2004).

CHAPTER 8: LUCID DREAMING, TELEPATHY, HEALING, AND OTHER POSSIBILITIES

PAGE 99. " 'The day before the disaster she . . .": Sam Knight, Burkhard Bilger, and
Louis Menand, "The Psychiatrist Who Believed People Could Tell the Future," *New
Yorker* (February 25, 2019). https://www.newyorker.com/magazine/2019/03/04/the-
psychiatrist-who-believed-people-could-tell-the-future.

PAGE 100. "Dreamers were to describe dreams of a target . . .": Robert McLuhan,
"Response Precognitive Dreaming Should Not Be Dismissed as Coincidence,"
Guardian (March 1, 2011). https://www.theguardian.com/commentisfree/2011/
mar/01/precognitive-dreaming-dismissed-science.

PAGE 101. "Once the sleeper was in the REM . . .": Stanley Krippner. "The
Maimonides ESP-Dream Studies," *Journal of Parapsychology* (March 1, 1993).
https://www.questia.com/library/journal/1G1-14527221/the-maimonides-esp-
dream-studies.

PAGE 101. "After she woke up, she still wasn't convinced . . .": Johnson, *Llewellyn's
Complete Book of Lucid Dreaming*, p. 305.

CONCLUSION

PAGE 105. "Rinpoche would indicate the world around . . ." Stephen LaBerge
and Howard Rheingold, *Exploring the World of Lucid Dreaming* (New York:
Ballantine Books, 2007), p. 67.

PAGE 108. "As the mystic Neville Goddard wrote . . ." Goddard, Neville. *The
Power of Awareness: Includes Awakened Imagination*. Mineola, NY: Ixia Press, 2019.

ACKNOWLEDGMENTS

This book would not have been possible without those who have done extensive work in researching and writing about lucid dreaming before me. First, thank you to my editor, Kate Zimmermann, who found me on the dream that is the internet and asked me to write this book. A big thank-you to Dr. Stephen LaBerge and to Dr. Clare Johnson for their work and research.

My interest in lucid dreaming led me down a lovely rabbit hole to reading works of other authors who studied consciousness and reality. I am indebted to Michael Talbot, who wrote *The Holographic Universe*; Dr. Elizabeth Lloyd Mayer, who wrote *Extraordinary Knowing: Science, Skepticism, and the Inexplicable Powers of the Human Mind*; Dr. Joe Dispenza, for his *Becoming Supernatural*; and the mystic Neville Goddard, who believed that God was imagination and by using our imagination we were all God. For somebody who grew up with absolutely no religion or beliefs other than in capitalism, money, and the American dream, I now firmly believe in the power of our consciousness to create our dreams and our waking reality.

I would like to thank my mother, Teresa Pei, for giving me life. I'd like to thank my father, Hung Chi Lee, and his wife, Rose, for all their support, as well. I owe a huge thank-you to my big sister, Iris, for her endless support and love, and all of my friends who have entertained my fantastical ideas about dreams and supported my longtime dream of being a writer.

Completing the writing of and researching this book while being confined during the global COVID-19 pandemic here in Paris has been a strange but rewarding experience. The outside world feels surreal, especially when projected upon us by the incessant and incendiary media. But writing a book on the power of lucidity has allowed me to focus on the beauty of life and all of the odd synchronicities that make life feel like a dream—life is a sweet dream, especially with my lovely companions Clément, Sésame, and Champignon.

INDEX

ABOUT THE AUTHOR

Cyrena Lee is a writer based in Paris and New York. She graduated from Barnard College with a degree in anthropology, and writes and thinks often about lucid dreaming, rock climbing, Late Capitalism, and spicy food. She has published work in *Club Sandwich Magazine* and *The Climbing Zine*, as well as short fiction in the anthology *Writing for Life*. She is currently working on editing a draft of her first novel and a collection of short stories. For more information or to write to Cyrena, visit cyrena-lee.com.